blind spots

blind | spots

achieve success by seeing what you can't
see

Claudia M. Shelton

BICENTENNIAL
1807
WILEY
2007
BICENTENNIAL

John Wiley & Sons, Inc.

Published by John Wiley & Sons, Inc., Hoboken, New Jersey.
Published simultaneously in Canada.

Wiley Bicentennial Logo: Richard J. Pacifico

For general information on our other products and services or for technical support, please contact our Customer Care Department within the United States at (800) 762-2974, outside the United States at (317) 572-3993 or fax (317) 572-4002.

Wiley also publishes its books in a variety of electronic formats. Some content that appears in print may not be available in electronic books. For more information about Wiley products, visit our web site at www.wiley.com.

Library of Congress Cataloging-in-Publication Data:

Shelton, Claudia Marshall.
    Blind spots : achieve success by seeing what you can't see / Claudia M. Shelton.
        p.   cm.
    Includes bibliographical references and index.
    ISBN 978-0-470-04225-0 (cloth)
    1. Success in business.   2. Executive coaching.   I. Title.
    HF5386.S42734   2007
    650.1—dc22

                                                            2006031238

Printed in the United States of America.

10 9 8 7 6 5 4 3 2 1

To Jim

Whose Support Makes All Things Possible

Contents

Preface

I WORKED FOR many years for Fortune 500 companies, being given increasingly larger management assignments in every function of the business. I loved the work and was lucky enough to be given the resources and support to develop new businesses and people in exciting ways. My business results were strong and recognized both in national business publications and through desirable board assignments. It was a wonderful period in my life for creative thinking and innovation. I thought I would continue my career like other MBAs climbing the corporate ladder.

But a time came when a voice inside my head told me I had a different purpose. I kept trying to say, emphatically no, but the voice wasn't silenced. After about six months, I found myself en route back to graduate school in counseling psychology. I had become intrigued with questions about why so many smart people I knew had made irrational decisions. Why did they bury their heads when change was imminent? Why did they cause conflicts that seemed so unnecessary to achieving their goals? Why did they treat themselves and other people in offensive ways? My purpose became "to understand how to help high-achieving, healthy people realize the full potential of their innate talents." My fellow graduate students and professors were skeptical: "That sounds like something worthwhile, but you'll never make a living at it!"

Maybe not, but I was passionate about trying.

As I finished graduate school, I began The Hopewell Group. What I had trained to become, I discovered, was now being called an executive coach. This was a new role for me, but I relished the change, and it's what I continue to do to this day. For 15 years, I've worked with CEOs, presidents, senior executives, and professionals from companies across a wide range of industries.

These clients helped me to see the broad applicability of my work to individuals at all levels of their organizations through seminars, group training, and leadership and motivational speeches. Word-of-mouth recommendations have taken me to help entrepreneurial start-ups, Capitol Hill, professional organizations, schools and universities, and businesses of all sizes. Other coaches and career counselors have asked for training in how to use this work to expand their businesses.

Recently, I asked a number of my clients if they could tell me what it was about my work with them that they found most important. Consistently, I received a similar answer: "You help me to see things about myself that I couldn't see before. Those things have made a huge difference in my success."

Hearing these comments, I couldn't help recall how skeptical my fellow students and professors had been about my dream. Somehow, I have helped my clients feel much better about themselves and be more successful in their work. As for the part I have played in their fulfillment, I feel like it comes down to one essential objective—I help them to see their *blind spots*.

When I first began to recognize people's blind spots, I thought they were just troublesome behaviors that needed to be changed for more constructive relationships. Over time I have realized that blind spots hide much more than nuisance habits. They are real obstacles that prevent us from using our strengths and hide our significant talents. They can derail careers. Once you get past blind spots, you recognize new ways of seeing the world that you never knew existed. Just *recognizing* a blind spot is like opening a window. Through that window, you can see yourself and other people in new ways, and with that clear sight comes the opportunity to launch significant new opportunities.

Uncovering blind spots releases potential. We get raises and promotions and learn to deal with difficult people. We get results and set meaningful new goals for success. We find better balance in our work and personal lives. We see new opportunities for our success whether we are beginning a career at 21 or emerging to a new career at 55.

All of us need to uncover blind spots, and it's an ongoing process. The behaviors that made us successful 5 or 10 years ago are unlikely to be effective today. Times change. Work requirements change. Behaviors that might have been impressive to a group of college students are not important to the boss who manages you at age 28. What brought you success as an individual contributor may not work to help you manage a group or build relationships with a new set of peers. What made you successful in the corporate world is likely to be quite different from what makes you prosperous and happy in the world of the entrepreneur. The very *meaning* of success at age 55 is different from its meaning at 40. Reality shifts over time, and when we don't recognize that shift, when we still think of success in old ways, we have blind spots.

Blind Spots: Achieve Success by Seeing What You Can't See tells the stories of numerous people whose lives have been changed using the principles, tools, techniques, and strategies that you find in this book. From the many clients I have worked with, I know that the steps I describe will help you, first, recognize your blind spots, and second, see past them to discover *today's* opportunities.

The book is organized around three simple focuses. First, the Five Principles of Clear Sight presented in Chapters 6 through 10 guide you to develop the perspective and mindset necessary to see things about yourself that you previously couldn't see. Second, once you begin to recognize your blind spots, you will find strategies in Chapters 11 through 17 that can help turn these blind spots into strengths that will build your success.

The third focus is on a set of tools that help you to identify personal information about *your* specific blind spots. These tools are identified in the section overview for each of the six sections of the book and are described in detail within the identified chapter. They are also found in the Appendix, for easy reference. It is my intention to provide a variety of tools, so each reader can select the ones that work best for their style of reading and learning.

By following the Principles of Clear Sight and using the customized tools, *you will be able to develop a strategy to turn your blind spots into strengths*. There is no saying how far this will take you, how much more you will enjoy your work, or how fulfilled you will feel when you take these steps. The changes can be dramatic. I've seen them happen. You face great opportunities in your future interactions with other people and in the career choices that lie ahead.

As you read this book, you follow an experienced route that will provide clear sight to your goals. You will see new possibilities for your own strengths, your relationships, and your future life!

Acknowledgments

THE BOOK COULD not have been written without the rich relationships I have shared with so many clients over the past 15 years. Their challenges and triumphs have inspired new ways to understand the role blind spots play in creating successful and satisfying work and personal lives. They have taught me to understand the real power of human potential. I have drawn from their stories with great respect for the confidential nature of our work together.

Others have been essential to bringing this material to publication. For over 10 years Marilyn Nemarich has urged me to share the principles and stories of this book. Our continuous conversations and her constant encouragement to move the project forward are greatly valued. Kaye Delano and Jerry Gross provided important guidance and support to move the concept into the proposal stage.

Laila Kain deserves special thanks. A talented writer and thinker, she has a way of appearing at the moments when I particularly needed thoughtful guidance. Her suggestions are always insightful and motivational, and I couldn't have completed the book without her.

Many people helped in the development of ideas at critical junctures. Jack Bergquist, Ed Faruolo, Maeve Ryan, Kay Clarke, Dale Lersch, Joyce Humphrey, Kathy Marshall, and Sean Cronin were all involved in discussing the evolution of principles and strategies. Kim Waltman helped develop cases and presentations that effectively demonstrate the principles. Paul and Kathy Connelly have collaborated on translating the concepts into practical survey tools.

My agent Ed Claflin has been an advisor on questions at all stages of book development and made important contributions to portions of the book. He is a delightful and high-spirited individual to work with, and I am grateful for his wisdom and experience.

No one could be more fortunate than I to have Laurie Harting as a senior editor at John Wiley & Sons. She brings vision and passion to her work and has been a constant and enthusiastic supporter of every aspect of the project, making significant contributions to what the book has become. Designer Michael Freeland was the talented creative spark who developed the book cover which brings *Blind Spots* to life. Brian Neill and other members of the Wiley team have always helped to make the project go smoothly. Midge Tilney, as well as the team from Cape Cod Compositors, gave careful attention to transforming the manuscript to print.

Special thanks must go to a group of believers who have been so generous in their personal support of me during this project, including Jayne Amodio, Ellie Crisman, Lori Petricone, Kelly Hayes, and Liz Perrin.

Finally, I must thank my husband, Jim Shelton, who is always there to support me. He accepted without question my absence for long stretches of writing, often quietly taking care of day-to-day issues that had to go on while I was hidden away with thoughts of blind spots. He indeed accepts my blind spots and brings clear sight to me every day of my life.

Section One

Unlock the Secrets of Your Greatest Strengths

Blind spots can be viewed as unconscious things we do that drive other people crazy. When that person is a boss, co-worker, client, or significant personal relationship, we may find our goals blocked and disappointments increasing. From this perspective, no one looks forward to talking about their blind spots, so we hold on to them and they keep getting in our way.

I prefer to think of blind spots as the doors to opportunities that we are not yet able to see. When we think of blind spots positively, we open ourselves to the vision we need to gain the clear sight necessary to understand our blind spots and turn them into strengths.

Chapter 1: See Blind Spots
Find out what blind spots really are. Learn how you can begin to see these things about yourself that you can't yet see.

- Use the *Five Most Common Blind Spots Framework.*

Chapter 2: Develop Clear Sight
Understand the simple approach that can turn your blind spots from vulnerabilities into strengths.

- *Develop a Clear Sight Plan.*

Chapter 3: Can You See What They See?
Do you think you have blind spots that others don't really see? Do others see blind spots you are not aware of? What blind spots exist that nobody sees?

- Use the *Priority for Handling Blind Spots Grid.*
- Develop your *Personal Self-Portrait.*

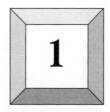

See Blind Spots

YOUR SUCCESS IS IN YOUR HANDS. Whether you seek a new job, a promotion, your own business, greater recognition, more social impact, a more balanced personal life, or any other goal, *you are the one* to make it happen. That's why recognizing your *blind spots* is so important. Blind spots are things we think and do unconsciously that can negatively influence how other people feel about us. Sometimes they are seen as irritating habits. At worst they can be tragic flaws that can derail your career entirely. For all of us, they diminish the possibilities we see for our success.

Nothing can erode your credibility faster than blind spots. While everybody else notices these distracting habits, you probably don't see them or you underestimate their effect. Yet they influence everything you try to do; every relationship you try to build; every goal you seek to achieve. If you fall short of success, think about whether it was a blind spot that led you to miss your target.

Blind spots was a term originally used to describe a small part of the retina of the eye that was insensitive to light and caused impaired vision. The term is now used widely in sports and other activities. When you drive your car, you are probably aware of your visual blind spot—the point where an approaching car gets lost in your rear view mirror. *Blind Spots: Achieve Success by Seeing What You Can't See* focuses on the type of blind spots that affect your success at work and in life.

Some initial observations about the sources of blind spots that can become visible in your relationships are:

- Every personal strength when overused has the potential of becoming a personal weakness.
- Every personal weakness when developed has the potential to become a personal strength.
- The environment we are in may influence seeing a personal characteristic as a strength or weakness.
- Different people may regard what we believe are our strengths and weaknesses very differently from how we do.

We can increase our level of self-awareness by asking others to help us see ourselves more clearly. I have found that those who become effective in recognizing and eliminating their blind spots are *those who learn just enough to take small steps to change their behaviors in simple ways on a consistent basis.*

The Liability of Being Unaware

Speaking to the top 150 managers of a high-tech company, I shared stories of people able to reach their goals only after eliminating blind spots. A vice president named Bill illustrated how work force diversity can influence the creation of blind spots. He was often recognized for his strength as a forceful, dynamic communicator. Believing all members of his group should share his sense of urgency, he sat down with one woman, who appeared somewhat tentative, to reinforce the commitment he expected. She said little, but he believed the meeting went well.

Several weeks later a colleague told him that the woman had experienced their discussion as "abusive" and was agitated enough to discuss it with others, who shared her point of view. Bill suddenly recognized that his forceful communication was the source of a blind spot. Different in style and background from others Bill had managed, this woman perceived Bill's style as demotivating and negative.

Like Bill, Janice is stymied by a blind spot. She is a talented, high energy, creative woman, whose manager thinks she's "high maintenance" because of conflicts she sets in motion. Janice doesn't understand why some people consider her style offensive and it annoys her that she has been identified as a "difficult person." What Janice doesn't see is that her way of gathering information quickly is to ask strong, direct questions. Others often find this approach somewhat jarring and conflict-producing. Janice believes she is simply getting to the core of the issue.

Surprisingly, the most common blind spot I see comes from misusing strengths. When Bill assertively communicated his expectations and Janice expeditiously gathered information, they were relying on strengths that had always served them well. However, in a new situation these habits were demotivating others. Personal awareness will enable both Bill and Janice to adapt their old strengths effectively to new situations.

In today's world *everyone* has blind spots. With the Internet, mass information, and the need to work on complex assignments in cross-disciplinary teams, there is always a variety of opinions regarding the perceived strengths of the same individual. We see this in the extreme in viewing political candidates, as the questions in the box below suggest. Successful people who have power and influence over others are often the recipients of other people's strong positive or negative emotions. Being unaware of how our behavior is interpreted by others can become a major vulnerability.

Political Blind Spots

How Do You See the Strengths of These Political Figures?

1. Does President George Bush's uncomplicated style of communicating make you see him as leaderlike or simpleminded?
2. Does Senator Hillary Clinton's professional speaking style make her appear highly competent or arrogant?

In his thought-provoking book *Blink*, Malcolm Gladwell reveals how a group of antiquities experts could determine a fake in an instant, while the same object studied by scientists and lawyers for nine months was believed to be real. The antiquities experts had perfected the skill of "thin-slicing"—knowing the very few factors that make a difference in an overwhelming number of variables. Over the course of my career, I have developed the skill of thin-slicing the factors that help others to fulfill their personal potential. My goal is *to make you a thin-slicer about crucial factors that affect your success, particularly recognizing your greatest strengths and related blind spots.*

Dennis Bakke, the past chairman of worldwide energy giant AES and author of *Joy at Work*, believes that the workplace should afford every person respect and the opportunity to experience the joy of using his or her innate talents. Paul Tieger, author of *Do What You Are*, demonstrates how our natural strengths suggest paths our careers will take for greatest personal satisfaction. I believe that recognizing blind spots provides an important method for continually understanding how our strengths can be best adapted to changing situations. Blind spots help us to understand aspects of our strengths that we may not yet have discovered, and provide signals of where we are not using these talents most effectively—a lesson that Joey, a 30-year-old salesperson, was about to face.

When Top Performance Is Not Enough

Joey was the top performing salesperson in his company. He believed that his greatest strength was his ability to engage and entertain people across his wide range of projects and situations. Throughout school he had been a class leader, captain of sports teams, and popular with girls. He had been in the top of his class at a well-ranked college. He had been the life of every party and could talk to anyone about anything. Now in his early thirties and working as a computer sales representative, Joey was certain he would be promoted. I met with him when he had been passed over for a sales management position.

When the district sales manager job had come open, Joey thought he had a lock on it. But another sales rep, someone slightly younger with not quite as good a sales record, got the job. Joey was angry and shocked. The decision made no sense. In his view, favoritism and politics made the difference. The company was playing it safe, he said. Management was just a bunch of "suits."

Up until this point, no one had given Joey any reason to believe he wasn't highly valued. In fact, even after he had been denied the promotion, managers up to the company president checked in to reassure Joey. They urged him not to take this decision the wrong way. They knew he was one of the best reps in the company, *but* they felt he needed a little more "seasoning" for a management role. As far as Joey was concerned, seasoning was meant for turkeys and he didn't intend to be eaten for lunch!

Joey shouldn't have been totally surprised by the missed promotion. In reality, his manager had cautioned him all along about his joking, missed meetings, and late reports. But Joey underestimated the importance of this feedback. *He thought it was petty in relation to his strong sales performance. He couldn't see just how disturbing his behaviors were to other people. He chose not to take the time to investigate more closely how these behaviors really affected other people's impression of him. In short, he decided not to be fully aware of what was required to meet his goals for success.*

A Perspective on Joey from His Boss, Hector

"Joey really knows how to reach our customers. He's our top national sales performer, and he has management potential. But I'm not sure he understands how to motivate people within our organization. Joey can be taxing. He needs to better understand what makes a team work well together, like doing the basics of coming to sales meetings, completing sales reports, and listening to other members of the group. He can't always be the star and center of attention. Quite frankly, our CEO has a finance background, not sales. He values marketing skills, but he wants managers who pay attention to the discipline of running a business. Joey needs to pay more attention to this side of the business if he wants to get ahead."

Joey's avoidance of facing his blind spots is not unusual. Most people choose to avoid confronting ineffective behaviors until a crisis or major disappointment comes along for two reasons. First, the behaviors reinforcing our blind spots are often formed in childhood and shaped by our early environment and relationships. They become habits that remain fixed in our adult lives. We are unconscious of their influence, and do not adapt these old habits to changing life situations. Like Joey we don't see them as a big deal, because they are so much a pattern in our routine that we can't imagine behaving in any other way. Like peanut butter and jelly, some combinations in life are always expected. Acting out our blind spots becomes so familiar that it feels like the only way to do things. Joey never questioned the value of how he approached his job, until he experienced this major disappointment.

The second reason we are able to ignore our blind spots is that other people do not like to give us negative news. It's easier and more fun to tell someone positive things; for example, Hector found Joey quite receptive to congratulations on his top sales performance. In contrast, while he recognized Joey's blind spots, Hector was reluctant to keep repeating negative feedback, particularly when Joey reacted with denial, blame shifting, and topic changes.

I had the opportunity to counsel Joey as he decided how to move forward from the missed promotion. His company really believed he had top potential, so they asked me to work with him to prepare him for the next management opening. Together, we worked on uncovering his blind spots and developing an action plan, which you'll find in the next few pages.

When we're not reaching a goal and we aren't sure why, we can get frustrated. It's not always easy to hear about our shortcomings. If we think others are seeing us unfairly, we can get angry or even start blaming. The whole subject of blind spots can make us feel tense or defensive. We can be extremely self-critical. However, to reach our goal and get to the heart of the blind spot, we need to shift our perspective away from these negative feelings and create space for our success. This is the most important step in overcoming blind spots. It is also sometimes the most difficult.

While he was still angry and thought his missed promotion was a failure on the company's part, Joey was committed to getting the next sales management position. He put all his effort into identifying his blind spots. Any time negative feelings would start to emerge, he pictured himself sitting in the next sales manager's desk, and took a deep breadth.

Joey needed to get information from his boss and others influential to the next sales manager decision. He met with each one, and carefully approached the subject, opening with, "While I am happy for Dan's promotion to manager, I have to say that I was disappointed not to get that chance. I want to understand what I need to improve to be considered for the next management opening." Joey used his excellent relationship skills to make the conversation easy and enjoyable.

The actual meeting with his boss was a different conversation from any Joey had ever had. He listened carefully to what his boss had to say and didn't interrupt or try to argue. His goal was to gather information about why he didn't get the manager job, not to change opinions. While he didn't agree with everything Hector had said, he left with a clear picture of what his boss saw as his shortcomings: He dominated conversations. His sales reports were often late or sporadically filled out. He sometimes came late or missed sales meetings. The management group saw Joey's behavior as an indication that he was lacking the discipline to take on broader responsibility.

In the process Joey gained new insight about how he had not been using his major strength, his relationship skills, effectively in relating to his boss and team members. He had been so focused on sales results with customers that he had simply ignored everybody else. As Joey paid close attention to his manager's comments, he realized "Hector has been trying to tell me for a long time to pay attention to things I didn't think were important. If I had been attentive, perhaps I would have that manager position now. I now approach him the way I would one of our customers. That has worked for me in the past."

Surprisingly, Joey found that as he got more information, he became less defensive. He just kept imagining that everyone was talking not about him, but about that "other person like him sitting in the room." As he slowly understood other people's perspectives, he began to see how he could use his strong relationship skills to turn this situation around. As he gained this self-awareness, his defensiveness seemed to evaporate.

Over time Joey would learn to see how his blind spots represent as-yet-untapped potential. They often result from our greatest strengths. To change them, we must develop an objective picture of how they work. When we build a model of our behavior, we can talk about ourselves in a simple and depersonalized way.

A Framework for Viewing Blind Spots

Through work with hundreds of individuals, groups of thousands, and re-views of quantitative assessment data from research validated instruments, I developed the Five Most Common Blind Spots Framework for thinking about blind spots. It provided a simple and objective way for Joey to summarize blind spot data he gathered.

Five Most Common Blind Spots Framework
Joey's Blind Spots

Misused Strengths	Too much "entertaining."
Old Habits	See being entertaining as "who I am," not just one of many skills.
Stress Expressed	Distracted behavior, for example, forgetting sales meetings and reports.
Untuned Radar	Missed need to listen to boss and others about what was important to them.
Disconnect	Overly talkative.

The framework enabled Joey to think objectively about which blind spots might be limiting his potential to become a manager.

1. *Misused Strengths: How ineffectively we use our strengths*
   Most people have certain personal, core strengths they often rely on in their work, for example, being a strong strategist, analyst, or relationship builder. The most frequent blind spot I see is someone *overusing that core strength.* Joey recognized that he overused his strength at being entertaining when he needed to use the skill of good listening.
2. *Old Habits: How we repeat outdated behavior*
   Old habits are the most difficult blind spots to uncover because they are ways of thinking and acting that have become fixed. Joey developed a pattern early in his life when he learned to get positive attention by using his talent as an entertainer. It was a charming, confident style for a high school boy. Joey has continued to rely on this skill in so many social settings that it is closely tied to the sense of who he is. This blind spot is not one that Joey was able to see at the start. To eliminate this blind spot, Joey needed to recognize that *this way of being in the world is not "who he is."*
3. *Stress Expressed: How we negatively express the stress we feel*
   We may think our stresses aren't visible, but unconsciously we communicate volumes. For example, some people who internalize their stress become self-critical and self-doubting, and they overcommunicate their shortcomings. They can appear overcontrolling, perfectionistic, or petty to others. At the other extreme are people like Joey. He realized that he doesn't feel stress very often, but he does transfer stress to others when he becomes disorganized or distracted. In these times he would forget about his sales meetings and sales reports.
4. *Untuned Radar: How we misread other people*
   Untuned radar relates to the inability to read other people's nonverbal cues. Some people read too much into nonverbal cues, which leads to misinterpreting others' intentions. Joey believed he was probably on the other extreme when he kept entertaining his bosses and peers when they wanted him to listen; he missed these cues entirely.

5. *Disconnect: How we fail to communicate*
   There are many ways our communication breaks down. Joey realized that he often tried to make a point by becoming overly talkative and not giving his boss and peers a chance to speak. This was the blind spot that blocked Joey from getting an earlier indication of his short-comings for the sales management role.

Having completed the Five Most Common Blind Spots Framework, Joey was ready to develop a Clear Sight Plan to turn his blind spots into strengths. Without this simple plan, Joey probably would have lost his focus in a few days. With it he managed a consistent effort to make the changes, which his boss and others began to notice.

Joey's Clear Sight Plan

1. Time Management
   Attend all sales meetings and hand in reports on time.
2. Listen/Contribute to Others
   Comment on positive contributions of team members and boss. Ask them questions at least three times a week. Program on calendar.
3. Special Project on Financials to Demonstrate Discipline
   Request special project. Discuss with boss in biweekly meetings.

We talk about Clear Sight Plans in detail throughout the book, but it's worth noting the simple approach that Joey followed. He immediately rectified the late reports and missed meetings by scheduling Black-Berry double reminders. He also scheduled time on his BlackBerry three days a week to focus on others by asking them questions about what they were doing, and then commenting actively about it in meetings. This was a little stilted at first, but it reminded him to stop entertaining and start focusing on the contributions of other people.

With practice, Joey began to do this without the BlackBerry reminders. Finally, he asked for a special sales financial analysis project from his boss so he could begin to demonstrate his competency in the disciplines of the business.

Joey's Perspective: How I Succeeded

*"I was really angry when I didn't get the sales management job. I couldn't be-
lieve the company could ignore my sales performance.* The good news is I just
got the next management opening. *How did I do it? The toughest part was
letting go of negative feelings and putting all my efforts into my goal of becoming a manager. I had to get my boss, Hector, to see that I could change the
things he saw as my weaknesses.*

*"It took some time to understand just what things bothered others. No one
wanted to give me the negatives. Using the Five Most Common Blind Spots
Framework helped me to organize my thinking.*

*"Basically, people thought I was too much into my own agenda and not
enough into that of the team. Hector didn't think I had the discipline to be a
manager. I told him what I was trying to change and asked him once a month if
he was noticing. His positive reaction motivated me to do more. It also improved the comfort level of our overall relationship.*

*"It wasn't easy. It took me a month just to believe I had blind spots. Blind
spots had locked me into habits I didn't even realize were limiting me. Once I
could see other perspectives, I started to make progress toward my goal. I made
simple changes in how I do things. This experience has changed my whole outlook on how I view my life."*

Be Proactive

Given the prevalence of blind spots in our society, why wait until yours
get in the way of your success? Companies that invest in developing their
future generation of leaders hire experts to work one-on-one with selected individuals who demonstrate leadership potential. Identifying and
eliminating blind spots goes to the heart of executive coaching.

One of the people I coached was a 40-year-old woman named Saundra, who was being elevated to a senior vice president position. Saundra's
boss saw her as a high-potential talent in his organization. He asked me
to coach her to insure her success as she moved from being an individual
contributor to managing a group. He told me, "She's terrific—smart, a

pleasure to work with, and knows how to get things done. She's got a lot of upside potential. I'd like to see her as our next head of global operations. I want you to help her to stay on course."

Saundra needed to discover the nuances of relationships with her boss, peers, direct reports, clients, and colleagues. By learning to thin-slice her blind spots, she believes she found the key to her recent promotion to running a group of 100 people.

The influence of blind spots is growing at alarming rates. We strive for speed in our lives. It gets us attention. We live on overload, have too many choices, and are often in a state of high anxiety—all of which make us prone to overuse our strengths and ignore our weaknesses. We are so much a part of the activity that we can't distance ourselves to see ourselves objectively. We easily fall into old habits that feel comfortable, and we grow accustomed to accepting our blind spots as normal.

One woman told me how she had sat at her desk contemplating for several minutes the possibility of giving a speech in Toronto and attending a meeting in New York within five minutes of each other. Of course, this is an impossible feat; however, she was so used to overscheduling herself that she momentarily spent time examining how it could be done. We can be so blinded by the frenzy that we don't see clearly.

Any person who works with or relies on others will find increased success by understanding and managing blind spots. I have helped corporate executives, entrepreneurs and educators, those in government, Wall Street firms, nonprofits, and even the self-employed learn how recognizing and eliminating their blind spots leads directly to greater effectiveness and its rewards. The earlier in your career you recognize and eliminate blind spots, the greater chance you have to keep them from interfering with your success.

As you read this book, you will have the opportunity to confront your blind spots head-on, perhaps for the very first time. It takes courage and an open mind. If you stay the course, you will learn to not only recognize your blind spots, but also learn to get the clear sight it takes to fulfill your potential for success. My goal is to help you to live and work *blind spot free*, relating to others in ways that help you to achieve your well-deserved success for life!

Strategies for Identifying Blind Spots

- Analyze yourself as if you were another person so you can depersonalize the process and be more objective.
- Always start by analyzing your strengths; this gives you a positive outlook.
- See your blind spots *not as weaknesses*, but as behaviors that get in the way of fully using your strengths.
- Gather information from others about what they see as your strengths and blind spots.
- Do not hesitate to ask people for information; the most confident people always ask for balanced feedback.
- Make it comfortable for people to share negative feedback with you. Be grateful for their help.
- If you identify several blind spots, prioritize which one you plan to work on first.

At the end of each chapter, I will ask you to answer one question for yourself. By keeping track of your answers, you will develop what I call a Personal Self-Portrait that will help you track blind spots over time.

Now you're ready for your first question: Think for a moment about how you define your greatest personal strength in your current work. How might you overuse that strength in a way that it creates a blind spot that could limit your success?

2

Develop Clear Sight

BLIND SPOTS OBSCURE your focus on any goal. You gain *clear sight* when you recognize your personal strengths for reaching that goal, identify any blind spot you have from overusing a strength, and strategize a simple plan to turn that blind spot into a strength. Developing clear sight is similar to solving a jigsaw puzzle. You look at all the pieces until you see an initial pattern that indicates how a group of pieces fit together. Then you look for more clues that lead to completing another part of the puzzle. Slowly you find a way to put each part together to complete the entire puzzle.

You don't have to see the whole picture of how your blind spot might be operating to gain clear sight. Once you have identified a potential blind spot, you can begin eliminating its influence. Those around you will start recognizing the results, which will motivate you to continue.

What often holds people back from facing their blind spots is the comfortable feeling of old habits. It just doesn't *feel right* to deal with others in new ways. The process of gaining clear sight can be experienced as a sudden insight or a slow increase in awareness such as:

- Behaviors, which reinforce blind spots, often feel familiar and comfortable.

17

- Recognizing a blind spot takes careful attention to small habits so you see them in new ways.
- The first step toward changing habits that reinforce a blind spot may *feel* awkward and risky.
- Actually implementing a small change in behavior is so easy that it will probably surprise you, given the feelings you had before doing it.
- Seeing other people change their responses to you in positive ways is very motivating and encourages further action.

As the blind spot fades and clear sight comes into focus, it's hard to imagine why you didn't make these small changes in habits sooner; they were so easy.

Commitment to recognizing and changing your blind spots is important to your success. As Arthur Williams points out in *The Success Principles*, it's essential to believe that what you want is possible, because the brain operates to *expect* what happens next based on previous experience. He tells the story of a study done on patients who believed they had had knee surgery but actually had received a "no operation." These people reported the same improvements to their knees two years later as patients who actually had had real surgery. What the brain *expected* actually happened. Such commitment and belief in the possibility of attaining one's goal is important to gaining clear sight.

The strengths that help us to achieve success as individuals may become blind spots when we need to rely on other people to accomplish our joint goals. Emma experienced this change when she received a significant promotion.

Emma Loses Self-Confidence

Previously a market research manager directing a three-person unit, Emma was named vice president of marketing for a group of 30 people. She had a track record of finding product breakthroughs with her strong, pragmatic analytical skills. In her new position, however, she was using these skills to overanalyze her own shortcomings. Losing confidence in herself, Emma noticed that several of those reporting to her appeared to be raising their eyebrows when she addressed the group. She felt unsure of herself as a leader and needed to find a way to regain her confidence. I met Emma as she was struggling through this transition.

Emma had been recognized as a star with this promotion, so it was difficult to go to her boss and say she felt overwhelmed. She thought about discussing it with her human resources representative, but that also seemed awkward. She decided to use the Five Most Common Blind Spots Framework summarized next to get some clues about the source of the problem before contacting anyone else. Emma noted her thoughts on paper so she could follow her thinking as she learned more about the situation.

Five Most Common Blind Spots Framework
Emma's Initial Self-Observation

Misused Strengths	Strong, pragmatic analytical skills when overused can lead to overly critiquing herself and the contributions of others in the group.
Old Habits	Is her inner critic over-operating?
Stress Expressed	Internalizes stress; becomes self-critical and self-doubting.
Untuned Radar	Perhaps overly sensitive to any negative cues from people in her group.
Disconnect	Retreats into herself; may communicate with uncertainty.

Using the framework as a self-awareness building tool, Emma was able to gain some important insights about her current situation.

1. *Misused Strengths: How ineffectively we use our strengths*
   Emma believed she was a strong analyst. She asked herself how she would appear if she was overusing her analytical strength and imagined herself overanalyzing problems. Was she being too critical?

2. *Old Habits: How we repeat outdated behavior*
   Emma wasn't sure about this one. She had often been told by friends and family that she was extremely self-critical and wondered if that could be a habit working against her.

3. *Stress Expressed: How we negatively express the stress we feel*
   Emma knew she internalized stress and wondered if that was increasing her self-criticism and self-doubt, as well as her criticism of the group.

4. *Untuned Radar: How we misread other people*
   Emma wasn't sure whether her self-critical feelings were being sensed by other people. Was Emma being overly sensitive about a few eyebrow-raising reactions from her direct reports? What was the real reason behind these reactions? Should she discuss these reactions with these people rather than assuming she was doing something terribly wrong?

5. *Disconnect: How we fail to communicate*
   Emma recognized her tendency to be introverted and retreat into herself. She hadn't discussed her feelings with anyone and even now was handling this problem all by herself. She might also be communicating this reticence to her staff. She realized it was important to find someone she could talk with.

With this initial information Emma was ready to develop her first Clear Sight Plan. She had already begun to gain clear sight just from thinking about the Five Most Common Blind Spots Framework. Her confidence started to increase as she describes next.

Emma's Perspective: Getting a Plan of Attack

"I was feeling a little overwhelmed going from 3 direct reports to a group of 30. I didn't want to raise people's concerns that I was over my head. Thinking through the Five Most Common Blind Spots Framework helped me to clarify what was happening. I was keeping my problems to myself and needed trustworthy people I could talk with.

"I spoke to my manager, Phil, about a coaching group for new managers at the business school I had attended. He encouraged me to try it. The group gave me a chance to talk with others in positions like my own. We all had thought through the Five Most Common Blind Spots Framework and had shared our conclusions. It was reassuring to find others struggling with how to handle similar problems. We helped each other find solutions.

"Phil also suggested doing an off-site meeting with my staff to get perspective on priorities. My direct reports were confident about their abilities to manage their projects but needed help in building relationships with senior people in their client organizations.

"With this input I could clarify my blind spots and develop a series of Clear Sight Plans to help me manage my new responsibilities. I felt more confident. I still have to work hard at not being so self-critical."

Three Steps to Clear Sight

It takes three steps to go from blind spots to clear sight. At first this will take time and effort. With practice you will be able to do it systematically in a few minutes or even seconds. I do it regularly once or twice a month when I review my important goals. In this way, I eliminate blind spots before they can affect my success.

Emma followed these steps to develop her first Clear Sight Plan, which will unfold as we go through these steps.

1. *Make a Model of Yourself*
   Examine your goals. Consider your strengths and ask yourself whether you might be overusing them for negative consequences.

Emma did this by completing the Five Most Common Blind Spots Framework. Other models are suggested throughout the book.

2. *Consider New Possibilities*

Gather information. Talk with someone who knows you or who understands your situation. It could be a colleague, friend, family member, or coach—someone who can test your thinking and give you fresh perspective. Emma did this by participating in a group of new managers at the business school she had attended. They compared their results in doing the Five Most Common Blind Spots Framework and discussed alternative actions.

3. *Take Simple Actions*

Commit to one, two, or three actions you will take to eliminate the blind spot. A few simple actions implemented consistently have far more power than an elaborate plan that you find difficult. Always set yourself up to succeed. Emma's first Clear Sight Plan reflected these three steps for clear sight.

Emma's First Clear Sight Plan

1. Participate in a seminar for new managers.
2. Hold an off-site meeting with the group to assess where to prioritize my efforts.

Emma began to feel more confidence simply by writing down her plan and recognizing that she was taking steps to accomplish it.

Quieting the Inner Critic

Emma recognized that her own inner critic was still getting in her way. She spoke with her manager about getting some additional help, and I was asked to coach her. I assured Emma that many of her feelings were very common to someone with significantly increased responsibility. The shift from being primarily an individual contributor to being a manager requires new skills, which she would build steadily over the next six months.

We talked at length about Emma's overactive inner critic. Throughout her life, she had been held to high standards. Her parents hadn't tolerated anything but As in school. This pattern had resulted in a blind spot that made Emma excessively hard on herself, sometimes even paralyzing her efforts. She recognized that her inner critic helped her to excel earlier in life but was now holding her back. I suggested that anytime she began to hear her overactive inner critic, she should thank it for its help and tell it to "go have an ice cream and play with the other children on the playground." This made her laugh, but it also seemed to quiet the critic. It is an excellent technique for transitioning the voice of an old habit into new behavior more supportive of today's reality.

To help Emma understand how her direct reports were viewing her transition into this position, I spoke with each one and summarized their common reactions for Emma. Denise's reaction, which was similar to that of others in the group, is noted in the sidebar.

Emma's direct reports had been experiencing the mixed signals that Emma was communicating. She was hypercritical of what they were doing, but seemed to hesitate in reaching out to build relationships with the people they considered their clients. She changed her direction in

---

Denise's Perspective on Emma

Denise is a direct report of Emma. Emma is a very smart woman and she knows what she is talking about. She hires good people and has high standards. But she keeps criticizing everything we do. We know what we're doing! Where she could really help is going out to build relationships and credibility with the senior people who head the departments we serve. It doesn't help us to have her sitting in her office going through reports.

At our off-site meeting, she seemed to hear what we all said about this. I'll wait and see what happens. It's important for her to build her own credibility with the senior people in the client organizations we serve if she wants to be seen as a player.

---

meetings and sent nonverbal cues that communicated uncertainty about decisions.

Emma was not surprised to hear this feedback. In fact, it helped her to understand how the feelings she thought she was having in private were being communicated to others in subtle ways. She was now able to develop a second Clear Sight Plan to address her inner critic and the mixed messages she was sending to her staff.

Emma's Second Clear Sight Plan

1. Quiet the Inner Critic
   Tell the negative voice inside my head to "go eat ice cream."
2. Keep Communication Short and Clear
   Schedule short meetings with tight agenda and clear goals. End promptly and set follow-up.
3. Watch Nonverbal Cues
   Check pitch of voice, eye contact, dress, and other nonverbal symbols of authority. Keep a daily journal of personal reactions noting hesitant behavior. Notice differences in communicating with staff versus client department heads.

The plan helped Emma to focus on a few objectives, rather than allowing herself to fragment her attention on every project going through her shop. For the time being, she gave the people who reported to her the chance to manage their projects with few recommended changes from her. She paid attention to establishing her authority within her group and developing relationships with client departments.

Emma kept meetings short and objective oriented. She was mindful of her own body language and attentive to cues such as the tone of her voice and her eye contact. For example, when she started to give someone an assignment and heard herself sounding hesitant, she quickly gave the assignment and set a follow-up date for a progress report. When her voice became too high-pitched, she would try and bring it back to a more mellow tone. Within a few weeks, she noticed that the eyebrow-raising behavior of staff members disappeared. She also felt more grounded and in control.

Emma also started setting up meetings with the heads of client departments. By asking her people to help her prepare for these meetings, Emma signaled this as a priority for herself. While she knew these meetings were of concern to her direct reports, she also wanted to establish a relationship for herself and her organization with these client organizations.

She felt awkward at first in the department head meetings. To help ease her anxiety, I suggested that she rely on her old strength of recognizing profitable new product trends. Emma's track record for producing new products was well-known and those in client organizations were always interested in her new thinking. This approach got her started on a positive note and helped her feel confident about discussing a broader agenda.

As Emma took the first step in recognizing and managing her blind spot, she began to gain clear sight. She was retraining her brain to a different set of expectations. She developed a habit of preparing a Clear Sight Plan once every six to eight weeks. That made her mindful of the blind spots that needed attention, so she could develop and program responsive strategies.

Clear Sight Is Easy!

I have been helping people to gain clear sight for 15 years and am still often startled by how easy people find it once they take the first step. I regularly hear, "I tried those first few behavior changes, and it wasn't hard." This sometimes leads me to observe, "That's great. We now know you have the skills. You just need to focus on when to use them in a new way." Simple steps, repetition, and focus create clear sight—not big changes and complex understandings.

How does it feel to gain clear sight? It's like waking up after a deep sleep. When your eyes begin to open, you may vaguely see the world around you in a very different way. You may even feel some pain diminishing. Now it's your turn to embark on this journey.

In the first chapter, you were asked to start to develop your Personal Self-Portrait by imagining one of your strengths and a potential blind spot. *For your next assignment, take that blind spot and think about one thing you can do to give yourself clear sight. It may be that you, like Emma, need to first talk to someone you know about this blind spot. If so, take the next opportunity to have that chat and see what perspective they can provide.*

As you read on, you can examine your goals and behavior from a very different perspective. You'll learn the skills and mindfulness you need to continually have clear sight. Consider what you really want carefully and be prepared to change your work and your life for the kind of success you've only dreamed about!

Can You See
What They See?

IT'S DIFFICULT TO know whether the person I feel I am is the one who others see. Joey in Chapter 1 believed everyone saw him as a likeable top-producer ready for management and was shocked to learn that others saw him as difficult to work with. Emma in Chapter 2 experienced a lack of self-confidence while others saw her as a micromanager with the wrong priorities. We often don't know how others think about us and others can't imagine the things we think about ourselves.

Marybeth, a product manager in the hotel business, imagined that her own blind spot was related to micromanagement. In talking to her staff, I heard no mention of micromanagement as an issue. They thought she was a good manager, except under stress when she sometimes became inflexible and stopped listening.

Pete had feedback from his manager that he was too harsh in dealing with others. Attempting to soften his style by sharing personal stories, Pete was energized by expressing this new side of himself. I talked with his peers, who told me that while they recognized Pete was warmer, they found his stories long-winded and too self-focused. He still had a way to go.

Recognizing blind spots and creating clear sight requires both self-awareness *and* feedback from others. It is an art *and* a science that takes some time to learn for several reasons:

- Most of us are not well trained to assess how we are affecting others.
- Often it's even difficult to know what we think and feel about ourselves.
- We don't know how to ask for feedback effectively.
- Others may be hesitant to give us negative feedback.
- We may have an outdated picture of ourselves.

These obstacles simply mean that we need a variety of ways to check for blind spots and to continually update our perspective.

Your Personal Self-Portrait

Stephen Covey, the author of *The Seven Habits of Highly Effective People*, points out that while we think we are objective in how we see the world, we are limited by the experience of our personal paradigm, a mental model of beliefs we learn about ourselves and our relationships with others. For example, do I see myself as outgoing and attractive to people? Am I a good conversationalist? Do people find me warm or reserved? Am I good at reading people's feelings? I prefer to call this model of beliefs about ourselves a *Personal Self-Portrait*, which was initially formed during adolescence when brain development first provided us the capacity to envision a picture of ourselves.

The time teens spend dreaming and listening to music is needed to develop their first perception of a personal self-portrait, which becomes a baseline sense of who we are. If we don't constantly update our adolescent perspective, we can be operating from an outmoded sense of who we are in a world pushing us to adapt to changing situations.

Our personal self-portrait can be a guide to self-awareness and a filter for information we receive about ourselves. Remember the story of Joey in Chapter 1. He experienced popularity as a teenager being overly engaging and entertaining. This became a belief in his personal self-portrait, which still influenced his behavior as a 30-year-old.

It's important to note that Joey's personal self-portrait operated largely *unconsciously*, which is true for most of us. Adolescent-age Joey found that other kids liked him when he was engaging, so he repeated this pattern. Not until he missed a promotion did he take the time to consciously reconsider these beliefs.

Through feedback from his boss and others Joey began to consciously recognize how the situations he faced at 30 required more sophisticated interpersonal skills than those of adolescent Joey. While being engaging was still a major strength, effective teamwork required additional skills such as active listening and not always expecting to be the center of attention. Shouldn't Joey have learned that at 14? Maybe, but Joey had been extremely popular and successful at 14. He simply had no reason to change.

How Do We Change Our Personal Self-Portrait?

Isn't it common sense that one will need more interpersonal skills at 30 than at 14? Through my experience in dealing with many highly successful people, I can tell you that *it is not so obvious*. I have coached many graduates of some of the top universities in the country who have never given this whole idea of changing their personal self-portrait any *conscious* thought. They certainly never recognized it as absolutely essential to their career success.

I remember being asked to work with Andrew, a 32-year-old hedge fund analyst. He had been in the top of his class at one of the top-rated business schools in the country and had chalked up an impressive individual performance record over the past eight years. Brilliant at developing and implementing investment strategies, he paid little attention to his interpersonal skills, much less this abstract concept of a personal self-portrait. After all, it's common knowledge that in the hedge fund business *only* investment performance matters. Right?

Once promoted to portfolio manager, however, Andrew was suddenly forced to deal with a team who often had major personal conflicts. The anger and shouting among traders, analysts, and administrators became so extreme that it gained the attention of the firm's partners.

Andrew suddenly realized that his personal self-portrait needed some adjustments if he was to learn to manage this madness without permanent damage to his career. He needed to develop his strengths not only as an investment manager but as a conflict manager.

Career development today requires attention well beyond image and job history. We need to know our ability to handle a wide range of interpersonal situations, have a firm sense of who we are in light of changing circumstances, and keep our personal self-portrait dynamic.

Trevor Gandy, vice president of human resources at the Chubb Group of insurance companies, refers to the "invisible" resume in contrast to the physical resume. While the physical resume records work his-

---

Image Is Not a Personal Self-Portrait

It's so easy to have a shallow image of oneself these days. Hollywood helps. Movies, magazines, DVDs, and all the electronic media provide so many pictures, impressions, and ideas. We can enjoy these fantasies and sometimes act them out. We absorb their emotional content. They seem very real. Of course, we know they are fantasies, but where does fantasy end and reality begin?

Certainly political image advertising helps to keep the boundaries blurred. We are offered powerful impressions of what it means to be conservative or liberal, Republican or Democrat. We know these pictures are oversimplified and manipulative. Yet they create symbols of beliefs.

When we don't have time to consciously think through the underlying beliefs, the images can be left in place and serve as substitutes. In the moment we are asked to make a decision, we return to the image and can retrieve our opinion. The brain helps fill in the gaps of the image and lets us feel we have a position when we've never really considered the facts.

Much the same process can happen when we think of an image of ourselves. We may have a superficial impression of who we are and how we act, but until we wrestle with how the image translates into the details of day-to-day life, we don't have a personal self-portrait we can believe in. We need to keep adapting that portrait to the challenges of everyday life. To be content with an untested image of ourselves is a recipe for failure.

---

tory, the invisible resume includes those things that indicate how you navigate the interpersonal workplace including communication and collaboration with people. Gandy points out that it is discussions about the invisible resume attributes that make a difference in significant career discussions with an employer—for both first time job applicants and those seeking promotion. Trevor now keeps a written record of his own previously invisible resume.

In *Working with Emotional Intelligence*, Dan Goleman draws on studies conducted in more than 500 organizations, which revealed that the skills that distinguish performers in every field from entry-level to top executives are those of emotional intelligence. This includes self-awareness, self-confidence, self-control, commitment and integrity, communication and influence, and the ability to respond to change. Star performers stand out over the long haul because they know how to manage change and conflict. These skills form the basis of the know-how that we can build into our invisible resumes and articulate for ourselves periodically to consciously update our personal self-portraits.

Which Blind Spots Require Your Action?

Some blind spots are simple to discover and act on. Other blind spots mark behaviors that cannot be accounted for within the scope of our current personal beliefs. Joey in Chapter 1, for example, thought his interpersonal skills were excellent because of the continued success he had achieved in sales. New information about his inability to work with boss and peers made no sense in light of his personal self-portrait. Simply, he could not reconcile the new information with the picture of the person he believed himself to be.

Gaining clear sight involves consciously reconciling the feedback we receive from others with what we believe about ourselves. Joey needed to broaden his understanding of the range of interpersonal skills required for his job and recognize where he had fallen short. He then had to develop these new skills, which in turn modified his personal self-portrait.

Section Two introduces a way to gather feedback from others so you can easily identify the gaps between how you believe you act and

	I See It	I Don't See It
Others See It	Box 1: Ready to Attack	Box 2: Need Other's Input
Others Don't See It	Box 3: Update Your Personal Self-Portrait	Box 4: Explore Discomfort

Priority for Handling Blind Spots Grid:
Who Sees My Blind Spots?

how others actually observe your actions—the area where any blind spots probably reside. The Priority for Handling Blind Spots Grid categorizes blind spots in terms of who sees them and who doesn't see them. It helps you prioritize actions necessary to gain clear sight.

Box 1: I See It/Others See It

This is the easiest blind spot to attack and usually arises when someone tells you that something you do is not working effectively. You understand what the individual is saying and appreciate his or her feedback. You believe the observations are reasonable and fit within your personal self-portrait. You simply need to modify your behavior.

One example is Sally, a systems analyst, whose team members seem to ignore her systems recommendations. One team member tells her that he thinks she has good ideas but talks so abstractly that he doesn't quite understand her. Sally accepts this observation. She knows she tends to think more conceptually than many of her co-workers. At the next meeting, she prepares visual aids to support her ideas. The team responds enthusiastically. Sally updates her personal self-portrait to recognize that she thinks abstractly and may need to use concrete visuals to better explain her ideas to concrete-thinking colleagues.

Blind spot eliminated. Clear sight found.

Box 2: I Don't See It/Others See It

This is a common blind spot that may take more effort to understand. You have a habit that is interfering with your relationships and you are totally unaware of it. Others see it and have tried to bring it to your attention, but you have ignored their advice. It is probably a blind spot that doesn't fit in your existing personal self-portrait.

Because any discussion of this blind spot is confusing to you and may make you anxious, you may become angry or hurt when others try to discuss it. You direct your negative feelings toward them and they learn to avoid the topic. Those who have a need for perfection or are sensitive to criticism are particularly vulnerable to this blind spot.

Nicholas had this type of blind spot. He knew he was an introspective thinker and tended to do his best planning alone in his office where he could carefully consider the quality and integrity of his work. This was part of his conscious personal self-portrait. Others read this behavior as Nicholas being sneaky and untrustworthy.

The blind spot didn't come to Nicholas's attention until a company sponsored 360° feedback questionnaire was conducted in his company and he received very low ratings from others on his trustworthiness. He was shocked and he asked me to help him figure out just what was going on. He needed to include others earlier in his planning process so they could understand and be a part of his thinking. He was not giving them sufficient time to understand and trust him. The relationship between early participation and integrity also required some rethinking in Nicholas' personal self-portrait.

Box 3: I See It/Others Don't See It

There are enough problems you have to face without inventing some for yourself! Here the blind spot probably lies in an out-of-date personal self-portrait, not in the reality of current relationships. In other words, something that was once a problem is no longer an issue. It can also result from too much introspection and not enough feedback from others. Re-examining one's personal self-portrait in light of current feedback can help to eliminate this blind spot.

Marybeth, who was sure her staff saw her as a micromanager, perceived this behavior as being problematic when indeed it wasn't a problem at all. She was unnecessarily holding an issue that was eating at her self-confidence. She needed to update her personal self-portrait and be pleased with her own progress. It's important to leave old ghosts behind.

Box 4: I Don't See It/Others Don't See It

So if nobody sees a blind spot, how can it exist? It may not; however, when relationships get uncomfortable for no obvious reason, you may be dealing with a blind spot that is hidden to both of you. Imagine that your boss requires you to cut back your expenses to the point that you have to fire someone in your group. It's not something he wants to do and he's done everything he can to prevent it. You feel guilty about this requirement and don't want to take any responsibility.

Unconsciously you place the blame on your boss. Your boss feels your resentment and doesn't know where it's coming from. Every meeting you have with your boss after that is uncomfortable, even about routine matters. A strain begins to build in your relationship, and neither of you can understand it. You have always worked so well together. You both assume that whatever is going on will pass.

Realize that when you feel uncomfortable or angry in the presence of someone for no apparent reason, there may be a blind spot at work. We discuss these types of blind spots in the second half of the book.

Conscious Choices

Is your personal self-portrait unconscious or outdated? Do you understand how people really see you? Do you have a particular habit or behavior that undercuts your credibility? I want you to have a *choice* about how you can most effectively work with other people to accomplish your goals and reach your desired success.

Having a conscious personal self-portrait that reflects who you really are today can make a difference in achieving your greatest success. If you complete the simple assignment at the end of each chapter, you will have completed a personal self-portrait by the end of the book. Keep notes on it. You will find this information helpful in developing your invisible resume. You will also understand the blind spots that undercut your success and how to eliminate them.

Before turning to Chapter 4, here's your assignment: Think for a moment about your personal self-portrait. Like most other people, you probably don't yet have it written down. But think hard about the one belief you have about yourself that you feel has been most important to your success in life so far. Hold that thought as you are introduced to the Blind Spots Profile.

Section Two

Discover Your
Blind Spots

There are many different kinds of blind spots. Section Two will help you to understand your core strengths and blind spots, the ones that come from the way your brain has been designed. When you operate from your blind spots, you are probably unaware of how you overuse your strengths under pressure in ways that don't support your current goals. Here you'll find out how to use them.

Chapter 4: Model Yourself
Develop an objective model of yourself to begin thinking about what you can't see.

- Use the *Blind Spots Profile* to self-identify your strengths and potential blind spots. Find more detailed descriptions of the nine *Blind Spots Profiles* in the Appendix.
- You can do the *Blind Spots Profile* online at www.whatsmyblindspot.com.

Chapter 5: The Way *They* See the Things You Do
You don't learn about your blind spots, because people don't want to tell you things that could hurt your feelings or make you angry. Silence is the preferred approach.

- Learn five different ways to comfortably get information directly from others about how they see your blind spots.
- One approach is a discussion format to follow in asking others *How Do You See My Strengths and Blind Spots?*
- You can also use the *Blind Spots 360* for a group in your workplace. You'll find it at www.whatsmyblindspot.com.

Model Yourself

ARE YOU READY to find your blind spots? Try taking the Blind Spots Profile. By answering questions in this chapter or doing it online at www.whatsmyblindspot.com, you'll be able to easily identify where your core strengths and *potential* blind spots may be hiding. Everyone has blind spots. My goal is for you to recognize their signs before they can interfere with your goals. Like a traffic light or a stop sign, they'll make you look twice so you don't get into an accident.

The Blind Spots Profile provides a simple model for starting a discussion about your core strengths and blind spots. This idea of a model is important. With the Profile, we will always be referencing *not you*, but *a personal model of you*. What is the difference? If I give you feedback about *you*, it can *feel personal*. When we talk about a model of you, we focus on a picture that we both can consider and share. You become, like me, a neutral observer for the moment. This is another step toward gaining clear sight and is important to acknowledge.

- Any talk about *your* blind spots may make you feel uncomfortable.
- By shifting our focus to the model, we depersonalize our focus on you.
- The model gives you an objective starting perspective, which you can adjust as you learn more.

- If the model provides useful information, you can incorporate it into the beliefs you include in your personal self-portrait; if not, discard it.

The point of the model is to give you the freedom to see yourself in a new way, not to critique you. So often in my work with high-achieving people, I see people looking for what's wrong. That's often not a useful mindset. I prefer to think about *what is possible*. What is it we don't see that can give us the clue to reaching our goals?

A Model to Meet Today's Pressures

Feeling constant pressure is typical for many today. One man said, "I work 50 hours a week in the office and bring work home. I am exhausted, but believe it or not, I am the slacker of my friends, some who work 80 hours and even pull all-nighters sometimes."

An effective way to cut through the stress and pressure is with good gut thinking. Malcolm Gladwell, the author of *Blink*, recognized that effective decision making creates a balance between deliberate and gut thinking. For example, a good car salesperson can read his customers quickly but also knows when to reconsider the facts of price negotiation.

When we are under pressure and don't have time to prepare, we use our core or *gut* strengths to get a quick read of what is important. Then we use our deliberate thinking to sort out the details and make decisions. Both parts of our brain work cooperatively together.

Many authors, educators, and psychologists have tried to explain the source of our gut strengths by developing categories of worldviews, such as the Myers Briggs indicator or the Enneagram. Sandra Seagal's work in Human Dynamics has looked at differences in our functioning as "whole systems."

My goal is not to create a system to help you analyze your view of the world. I want to give you a *simple starting point* to recognize patterns of gut strengths and related potential blind spots. In working with clients, I have found it easiest to discuss these patterns by observing how we *Quick Think* and *Quick Feel*, the two dimensions of the Blind Spots Profile.

Quick Thinking

When there is information all around us, our gut strength steers us to focus on particular pieces of information that give us a quick read of what is going on. Some observe what I call *Feelings First*; others focus on *Ideas First* and a third group focuses on *Instincts First*.

Feelings First

Feelings First gut thinkers scan personal feelings of others in an instant. Aware of positive or negative emotional reactions, they quickly recognize shifts in the emotional environment. Feelings first gut thinkers are not necessarily emotional people. They simply read a person's feeling reactions easily. They are usually perceptive processors of emotional information.

For example, a feelings first advertising executive can look at a series of ads and have an inner sense of a target audience's probable emotional response. Looking quickly at five possible ads, one ad exec pointed out the one that she "knew was right" for the audience. Later research reiterated that this was indeed the best choice. Through her feelings first thinking, this woman carried an impression of a preferred emotional reaction.

Ideas First

Other people recognize *Ideas First*. They quickly observe the natural structures in relationships of people, recognize tensions between objectives and desired goals, and see necessary boundaries for goal accomplishment. They become instantly aware of rules or structure that needs to be in place to make things happen. They notice when a system is not clearly defined to support its goals. They recognize natural principles of organization.

One ideas first gut thinker was negative about a qualified individual being considered to serve on a board of directors. The individual held a position that could create a conflict of interest with issues the board would be wrestling with down the road. Others on the board felt more comfortable about the individual joining the board now and worrying about potential conflicts later. The ideas first gut thinker observed these boundary issues far in advance.

Instincts First

Instincts First gut thinkers scan the environment for sensory information. They observe small details of verbal and nonverbal cues, and have constant attention to the presence of people in the room: where they sit, how they talk, what they say and don't say, their clothing, posture, and readiness to attend to what is going on. From these observations they determine what is out of sync about someone's behavior, and why. While feelings first people relate to feelings of people, instincts first gut thinkers relate to the capabilities and operational nature.

For example, one instincts first individual tells of coming into an investment meeting and noticing a small detail—a man who usually made coffee hadn't done so. She watched him further to see his openness to discuss certain issues and believed he was hiding something. She slowly became aware of a pattern of responsibilities this man hadn't followed through on and found out he hadn't fully completed the investment responsibility he had been assigned. Instincts first thinkers have an uncanny sense of knowing who did something right or wrong without first knowing any facts.

Quick Feeling

How we choose to process the gut information we have acquired is what I call *Quick Feeling*. Some like to *tell* others about it and better understand it while stating it. Others like to discuss it with someone else and the third group prefers to process it within themselves.

Extroverted

Extroverted gut feelers like to present ideas to others and are comfortable being the center of attention. They process information by talking out loud, and will be the first to repeat what they learn from their gut thinking. Talking out loud helps these people to integrate the new information into what they already know. Others may observe these people "talking to" rather than "talking with" others.

Introspective

Introspective gut feelers like to absorb their gut-thinking within themselves to further process it and get an inner sense of its meaning. They have an ongoing inner dialogue, which they may or may not choose to share with others, who observe them "not talking." For this reason, their behavior may be somewhat surprising to others at times. They tend to explore the implications of new information more privately and intensely than others.

Interpersonal

Those of the *Interpersonal* style are neither extroverted nor introspective but tend to work in between these styles. Others often observe these individuals in conversation with people. Interpersonal gut thinkers like to interact and engage others in a give-and-take dialogue to process their gut thoughts. It is through the interaction that this information gains meaning.

Identify Your Blind Spots Profile Model

Think for a moment about which of these gut-thinking approaches and gut-feeling approaches are the ones you use. Now look at the Blind Spots Profile Matrix and find the box that matches both your selections. If you are uncertain, you may want to mark two or three boxes that you think could represent your style of quick reacting.

Quick Thinking Style

	Read Feelings First	Read Ideas First	Read Instincts First
Extroverted	Optimistic Image-Oriented Producers	Energetic New-Direction Risk Takers	Assertive Get-It-Doners
Interpersonal	Warm Relationship Builders	Practical Questioning Loyalty Builders	Responsible High-Standards Builders
Introspective	Sensitive Perceptive Creators	Reserved Analytical Strategists	Empathic Conflict-Avoiding Diplomats

Quick Feeling Style

Blind Spots Profile Matrix

Each of these nine Blind Spots Profile models possesses both a unique strength and a potential blind spot, which occurs when that strength is overused. When we are respectful of the strength and use it in a balanced way with our deliberate thinking, we will effectively use our personal strengths for constructive purposes. When we allow ourselves to be over-stressed and emotionally distracted, we can move into a blind spot where our gut strength can work against us.

The following chart summarizes the gut strength and potential blind spot of each model. We refer back to this chart often throughout the book to begin discussions of the strengths and blind spots of many individuals at work in different situations. It's a blind spot conversation starter.

Blind Spots Profile

Strengths and Potential Blind Spots

Optimistic Image-Oriented Producer (page 224)

Greatest Personal Strength: High-energy multitasker produces many projects valued by others.

Potential Blind Spot: Constant multitasking can lead to disorganization and indecision. When pressured can become distant, dismissive, and alienate others.

Energetic New-Direction Risk Taker (page 225)

Greatest Personal Strength: Constantly initiating new ideas. Enthusiasm creates energy and excitement.

Potential Blind Spot: Lack of self-disciplined follow-through on ideas can lead to failure. When feeling boxed in by structure, can become irritable, blaming, and lose memory of recent events and decisions.

(continued)

Blind Spots Profile (*Continued*)

Assertive Get-It-Doner (page 226)

Greatest Personal Strength: Knows how to get big things done.

Potential Blind Spot: Can become too confrontational or bossy. When unappreciated can become suspicious and mistrustful.

Warm Relationship Builder (page 226)

Greatest Personal Strength: Innate understanding of the feelings and needs of others.

Potential Blind Spot: If feelings not reciprocated appropriately, can focus on personal shortcomings and withdraw. Can try to avoid negative feelings by becoming manipulative.

Practical Questioning Loyalty-Builder (page 227)

Greatest Personal Strength: Uses intellect to test the dependability and trustworthiness of people and ideas they work with.

Potential Blind Spot: Can work so hard to test the trustworthiness of a person or organization that they lose confidence and put off decisions. Analysis paralysis results.

Responsible High-Standards Builder (page 228)

Greatest Personal Strength: Innate self-discipline and standards for doing the "right" thing.

Potential Blind Spot: In pursuit of goals can become too serious and overly responsible. Can become distant, angry, aloof, and inflexible when too focused.

Sensitive Perceptive Creator (page 229)

Greatest Personal Strength: Uses perception to find unique, creative ways of contributing to others and understanding the emotional needs and states of people and organizations.

Blind Spots Profile (*Continued*)

Potential Blind Spot: Can become too emotionally focused and ignore social expectations. Can overwork and become ill.

Reserved Analytical Strategist (page 230)

Greatest Personal Strength: Insightful methodical ability to see both forest and trees.

Potential Blind Spot: Can move too much into the head and become distant and aloof. When pressed can become distracted and dictatorial.

Empathic Conflict-Avoiding Diplomat (page 231)

Greatest Personal Strength: Uses perception to "walk in the shoes" of others and understand their needs. Makes excellent facilitator to bring a group together.

Potential Blind Spot: Can become lost in other people's needs and ignore their own. Avoids negative feedback.

Most people usually relate to two or three of these models. Think back to your adolescence and see which model describes a picture of your at that time, for that is probably closest to your natural gut strength. Other gut strengths were probably developed to face certain life situations. If you are not sure which model represents you the best, look at the longer descriptions of each model in the appendix. You may also want to complete the questionnaire available at www.whatsmyblindspot.com, which will identify the top two models that apply to you and provide rankings of how you scored on all the models.

Before completing Chapter 4, note the one or two models that you see as your best fit. Be sure to record your gut strengths and possible blind spots so you can refer back to them as we consider the stories of other people presented throughout the book. Note the models in your developing personal self-portrait.

Chapter 5 helps you to understand how others see your strengths and potential blind spots. By comparing your Blind Spots Profile with what you learn in Chapter 5, you'll see which blind spots require your immediate attention.

The Way *They* See
the Things You Do

HAVING IDENTIFIED YOUR gut strengths and blind spots in Chapter 4, you are ready to get information from others about how they see your strengths and blind spots. If you think talking with someone about your blind spots sounds like the last thing you'd like to do in the world, realize you are not alone. I have met company presidents who invest millions of dollars without a thought but wince at the idea of asking someone about their blind spots. There are a number of reasons why talking about blind spots is difficult:

- Most people try to avoid giving negative feedback to others.
- Many don't want to make you feel badly.
- Many are afraid that if they deliver negative news, you'll "shoot the messenger."
- Many are afraid that if they give you bad news, you'll give them bad news back.
- High achievers seem to naturally prefer to hear praise and adulation.

To overcome these obstacles, you have to develop an approach that fits your way of doing things. You want other people to consider it routine for you to ask for this type of information. I'm going to give you five different approaches so you can choose one that will make this process seem natural for you. The first two approaches can occur in the course of a regular conversation.

The last two approaches I share rely on the Blind Spots 360, which is available for group use online at www.whatsmyblindspot.com. It provides information that can be compared to the Blind Spots Profile results.

Approach #1: Getting Balanced Feedback

This first method is simply a good communication practice. Build a habit of getting balanced feedback regularly so your asking for constructive feedback is not unusual. For example, when you've finished a project or given a presentation, say to your team members, your boss, or a colleague: "Before we conclude, I'd like to get some balanced feedback. What went well in this project? What might we want to change if we did it again?"

Make a habit of asking this type of question at the conclusion of any work you do with others. People will see it as your signature style, and will trust that you really want to hear what they have to say—whether it is good or bad. For example, if you tend to be wordy and talk too much, ask questions like, "How was the length of the presentation? Did I say too much about _____ ? If I did this presentation again, do you think I should cut back on the points I made about _____ ?"

This conversation just makes good common sense. People will see it as evidence that you are receptive to their ideas. They may at first be hesitant to share their more negative reactions but will eventually believe that you really want to hear what they think. And importantly, they will feel that it is normal to assess things from multiple points of view. The more regularly you use this type of questioning, the more honest people will become as you welcome their reactions.

Some of the very best leaders I have worked with are ones who have made getting balanced feedback routine. To improve and keep their edges, they need to know what they are doing or not doing that deserves priority attention. Welcoming both positive and negative feedback communicates self-confidence about yourself to others. It is also a sign that you value what someone has to say. You may not agree with it, but you want to always be looking for any blind spots that may be blocking your success.

How Joey Took the First Step

The benefits of getting balanced feedback are clear. But how do you begin this conversation? Go back to the Blind Spots Profile you selected in Chapter 4, and use that information as the backbone for your conversation. For example, remember Joey, the top-producing salesperson in Chapter 1 who missed promotion to sales manager the first time around. By completing the Blind Spots Profile in Chapter 4, Joey recognized his personal model, which follows.

Joey: An Optimistic Image-Oriented Producer

Greatest Personal Strength: High-energy multitasker produces many projects valued by others.

Potential Blind Spot: Constant multitasking can lead to disorganization and indecision. When pressured can become distant, dismissive, and alienate others.

How did these strengths and potential blind spots appear to others? Using his high energy to build sales, Joey assumed his performance alone would endear him to his company's management. Operating from a blind spot, he ignored his relationship with his boss and fellow salespeople. Under daily stress, Joey became disorganized in the office, missed sales meetings, and was late with sales reports. While Joey was charming in recounting customer stories, he appeared distant from his boss and peers when he had to attend sales meeting. They found him difficult to work with in spite of his success in the field.

When Joey knew none of this, how could he have obtained this information? With the knowledge of his potential blind spots he would have gained from taking the Blind Spot Profile, Joey might have said to

Hector, "When I get pressured, I sometimes get distracted from priorities. I just wanted to see if there was anything I'm not doing that you think is important." Hector would have pointed out the missed reports and meetings. Joey, knowing of his potential blind spots, would probably have done something about it.

After missing his desired promotion, Joey regularly asks for feedback about how he is supporting the team. For example in a two-minute conversation with his boss during his biweekly review meeting, he says, "Hector, I just wanted to get some balanced feedback from you on how I contributed to the last sales meetings. Was I helpful? Were there some ways that I should have been paying more attention to Joshua or Amy? Am I getting all my administrative bases covered with the right reports at the right time?"

The important part of this quick conversation is that Joey has created a moment for mindfulness for both himself and Hector. Just by taking that step, Joey is establishing clear sight. The disorganized and distant behavior that Joey had unconsciously created has stopped. As Joey repeats the habit of getting balanced feedback on a regular basis, he keeps blind spots in check. Joey admits that this routine is really easy and saves him time in the long run. He can't imagine why he didn't do it sooner.

We'll look at how people representing other Blind Spots Profiles are obtaining feedback in other ways. Before leaving this first approach, let's look at one more case, the story of Safron, whose personal model is a Reserved Analytical Strategist, whose strengths and blind spots are summarized next.

Safron: A Reserved Analytical Strategist

Greatest Personal Strength: Insightful methodical ability to see both forest and trees.

Potential Blind Spot: Can move too much into the mind and become distant and aloof. When pressed can become distracted and dictatorial.

In contrast to Joey, who had an extroverted feeling gut-strength, Safron is more introspective. She disappeared into her office whenever she was assigned a new project. While this time away supported Safron in developing extensive concept plans and strategies, her staff felt she was not giving them important information that they needed to do their jobs.

Realizing from taking the Blind Spots Profile that her potential blind spot distances her from others, Safron is careful to regularly get balanced feedback. Periodically she asks staff members whether she is providing sufficient communication and support. She follows a similar line of questioning with peers on other project teams, questioning whether she is giving them enough time for discussion about joint goals. She is direct in clarifying that the time she spends alone is helpful in developing strategic direction for important initiatives. But she also reinforces the importance of their input. Since Safron appears to be such a reserved person, people appreciate this personal connection she tries to build. Very disciplined in her habits, Safron regularly practices the balanced feedback strategy for clear sight.

This first approach works well when you have a good idea about where your blind spots might show up, and want to check whether or not you have the clear sight to manage them.

Approach #2: Informal One-On-One Discussions

Remember the Five Most Common Blind Spots Framework introduced in Chapter 1? This serves as another useful template for identifying blind spots in discussions with someone else. Go back to Chapter 1 if you want to review the process Joey went through in thinking about the framework. We also use it again later in the book. It's summarized in the box on the next page.

Through a one-on-one discussion with a helpful colleague or possibly an ex-boss, you can discover if any of these common blind spots are showing. If you're going to try this approach, I recommend you first go through the questions in the Discussion Format and answer them for

---

The Five Most Common Blind Spots Framework

1. Misused Strengths: How ineffectively we use our strengths.
2. Old Habits: How old patterns of behavior get in the way of to-day's challenges.
3. Stress Expressed: How we negatively express the stress we feel.
4. Untuned Radar: How we misread other people.
5. Disconnect: How we fail to communicate.

---

yourself. Based on your past experience, where do you suspect your gut strengths and blind spots might be hiding in your present situation?

Second, pick a couple of people you feel comfortable talking with like an old friend, a colleague, or even an ex-boss. Sit down and talk with them about these questions and ask for feedback about how they see your strengths and blind spots.

Finally make note of any areas of agreement or disagreement about your strengths and blind spots. You may want to talk with someone else about this particular information.

The discussion guide on the next page provides some questions you may want to explore with someone else. Use it as is or adapt it to ask the questions you see relevant.

How Alan Got a Fresh Perspective

Let's walk through an example of how Alan used this discussion guide to identify troublesome blind spots in his relationships. When I met Alan, a new product development manager, I suggested that he try this discussion approach. He was feeling frustrated in his job and wanted to get some information about how others saw him.

Alan had gone through three jobs for three different companies in four years. He knew he interviewed well but didn't seem to be able to stay satisfied with a job for more than a short period. He wondered if this behavior might involve a blind spot. He knew while he loved the oppor-

Discussion Format: How Do You See My Strengths and Blind Spots?

1. What do you see as my greatest personal strength?
2. What do you see as my greatest personal strength in relationships?
3. In terms of how I handle stress, is there anything I do that creates more stress for others?
4. If we met for the first time, what impression would you have of me before I had said a word?
5. Some people read information very quickly. Have you noticed how I grasp information? (e.g., gut reactions, intuitive feel, getting a quick overview). Have you noticed any ways that I miss nonverbal information?
6. In terms of my communication with other people:
   - Am I approachable?
   - How do I engage others?
   - How do I manage differences of opinion?
   - Do I recognize contributions of others sufficiently?
   - Am I socially and politically aware?
7. Are there any blind spots you think I may not see about myself that affect my relationships with other people?

tunity to suggest new ideas, he found the detailed reporting process cumbersome and boring.

Before talking with others, he decided to take the Blind Spot Profile and found these results:

Alan: Energetic New-Direction Risk Taker

Greatest Personal Strength: Constantly initiating new ideas. Enthusiasm creates energy and excitement.

Potential Blind Spot: Lack of self-disciplined follow-through on ideas. When feeling boxed in by structure, can become irritable, blaming, and lose memory for recent events and decisions.

Alan thought the results made sense, although he was surprised that one of his potential blind spots was related to blame shifting. He was beginning to get clear sight. I thought that he would gain more insight by getting feedback from others who knew him and that Alan would be very comfortable with this approach. He was ready to use the discussion format.

Alan selected different people who had known him in previous jobs to have lunch with him one-on-one. He asked each person to help him reflect on his personal strengths and possible blind spots. Alan found this whole approach exciting, and communicated his enthusiasm to his luncheon partners. They were intrigued.

As he slowly asked the questions from the discussion format, he got similar answers from the various people. His strengths were in creating excitement for new idea development. He created stress on others by dropping responsibilities on them and then changing directions. Irritated when he had to talk constantly about details of implementation, Alan would attack those who reported to him for no apparent reason. He would shift blame when things went wrong to others for his own failures. He communicated energy and adventure, but totally ignored negative reactions of people who worked for him. Slowly his organization would fall apart beneath him.

Notice how the information Alan got from others was reinforcing the results of the Blind Spot Profile. Slowly Alan also recognized this connection.

Alan now realized that his frustrations could not be blamed on others, but on his own difficulty in initiating too many new directions without providing the structure to implement them. He also recognized that his pattern of staying in jobs for less than two years was probably related to his inability to do something about his blind spot. Alan needed to find ways to support his exciting ideas in ways that valued the people reporting to him. To sustain his position, he needed to find a way to work with implementation as well as idea generation.

Approach #3: Use the Blind Spots 360 Feedback Tool

If the idea of talking with someone about your blind spots still seems awkward, you may find the Blind Spots 360 helpful. This is also useful for someone who wants baseline feedback. Designed with a report organized around the Five Most Common Blind Spots Framework, a sample of the issues explored is displayed in the Blind Spots 360 Report Topics chart that follows. The tool can be accessed for use by a group at www.whatsmyblindspot.com. You will be able to get feedback from yourself plus between 3 and 15 other people.

Blind Spots 360 Report Topics

1. Greatest Strengths: Are your strengths consistently recognized?
   - What do others see as your overall strengths?
2. Old Habits: Are old patterns visible?
   - Are there any old habits showing that interfere with your goals?
3. Stress Expressed: How do people see you acting under stress?
   - Are you calm, distracted, composed, or fearful?
   - Do you communicate resilience?
   - Are you irritable and critical, or indecisive and procrastinating?
   - Do you become overly accommodating and reserved?
   - Do you manage time effectively?
4. Tuned Radar: Do you read other people? What resonance do you communicate?
   - What does your presence convey to other people without your saying a word?
   - How effectively do you read nonverbal information?
5. Connection: Do you communicate effectively?
   - Are you approachable?
   - How do you engage others?
   - How do you manage differences of opinion?
   - Do you recognize the contributions of others sufficiently?
   - Are you socially and politically aware?

I thought the Blind Spots 360 could be a helpful tool for Barry, the president of a mutual fund company. At 35 he had been developing as a manager for more than 10 years and was at a point where he felt he was no longer growing professionally. He wanted to get fresh feedback to use in setting new personal development goals. He first decided to complete the Blind Spots Profile, which revealed Barry's gut strength and potential blind spot as summarized next.

Barry: Responsible High-Standards Builder

Greatest Personal Strength: Innate self-discipline and standards for doing the right thing.

Potential Blind Spot: In pursuit of goals can become too serious and overly responsible. Can become distant, angry, aloof, and inflexible when too focused.

Barry also wanted to get an overall reading on how other people saw his blind spots using the Blind Spots 360. He sent the tool to 10 people including his boss, six direct reports, and three people he works closely with from other businesses. All but two of them completed it. The summary results showed that he was a lot tougher on himself than others were. Respondents saw him as a good manager, who builds his organization consistently over time. He was seen as a good communicator, whose only real blind spot was his negative perspective: He sees the "glass half empty," always recognizing what was going wrong. Under pressure he became even more critical, irritable, and worried. They wished that sometimes he would try telling them what he valued in what they were doing, not just the negatives.

The survey respondents felt that these negatives limited Barry's capacity for strategic planning. He often rejected possibilities that others thought could have future competitive potential. While overall he was seen as a strong manager, his seriousness and inflexibility could be demotivating to others around him.

Barry was pleased to get a fresh perspective and asked me to help him work on his blind spots.

As you'll see in Approach #4, a coach is also another helpful way to get feedback in certain circumstances.

Approach #4: Have Someone Else Ask

If you need some feedback and find it difficult to be objective, you may want to hire a coach to get feedback from others for you. This is a popular method used by corporations as a development approach for managers who are moving into new jobs or working in areas outside their established expertise. Corporations usually pay for this resource and see the value in hiring a coach over a period of three to six months to support their top talent.

Gloria, an aerospace engineer, was the object of much water cooler talk. She was thought of as too aggressive and confrontational in her direction to others. Gloria's boss told her about this since others were afraid to tell her directly for fear of retribution. Gloria was surprised by the feedback and wanted to understand it more in depth. She took the Blind Spots Profile, which confirmed that her blind spot often showed up in being too bossy and confrontational. The Profile results are summarized next.

Gloria: Assertive Get-It-Doner

Greatest Personal Strength: Knows how to get things done.

Potential Blind Spot: Can become too confrontational or bossy. When unappreciated can become suspicious and mistrustful.

Gloria wanted to get more details about people's perceptions of her. Since people were afraid to talk with her for fear of a harsh, suspicious response, Gloria ruled out the direct discussion approaches.

She took the Blind Spots 360 and hired me as a coach to help her get more information. The Blind Spots 360 helped me to develop questions to ask in half hour discussions with six people Gloria had identified. I was able to ask for examples of the behaviors pointed to in the

Blind Spots 360. With this accumulated feedback, I helped Gloria develop a Clear Sight Plan, which I share later in the book.

The last approach to getting feedback from others uses elements of the first four approaches to create a group discussion.

Approach #5: Try a Group Discussion

For those who have some comfort in understanding their Blind Spots Profile and who have completed the Blind Spots 360, a group discussion can provide a useful way to get further feedback. Such a discussion could include all the members of a work group, people who share similar personal models, or simply a group of people who want to learn more about their blind spots. This is an excellent approach for a group of people interested in their career development needs.

Josh met Mary and Keiko in the same evening business school classes. In their Organization Development class, they had each completed the Blind Spots Profile and Blind Spots 360. Josh recognized from the results that he had difficulty giving and receiving negative feedback. In talking with Mary and Keiko, he discovered that they all worked for extroverted style bosses, who were far less introspective than these three. Mary and Keiko recognized that they, too, were sensitive to both receiving and giving negative criticism. These three people were highly empathic and easily took negative criticism to heart.

They found it useful to share examples of how to deal with difficult people. In their empathy they found shared strength. They began to share ways they felt comfortable standing up to others to lower their own stresses, and better manage their time. The fact that they came from different companies made them feel comfortable sharing personal incidents without fear of their stories getting on the grapevine. This group was moving their discussion from finding blind spots to implementing ways to get clear sight.

Before moving to Chapter 6, do one simple task: Talk with one individual about how they see your blind spots. This could easily result from discussing the results of your Blind Spots Profile with a friend. The important part is to get their views about you, and be comfortable in the discussion. Add this information to your developing personal self-portrait.

Now that you have some ideas about where your blind spots lie, you're ready to move forward to Section Three, the Five Principles of Clear Sight. These five principles will help you to get the perspective and attitude critical to seeing your blind spots in a way that will help you turn them into strengths.

Section Three

The Five Principles of Clear Sight

In working with over a thousand people, I have noticed the difference between those who are able to see their blind spots and reach their goals and those who get stuck in their blind spots. The successful group develops the positive mind-set to see new opportunities for themselves.

Chapter 6: Clear Sight Principle 1—Shift to Neutral
Let go of the anger, blame, and withdrawal that sometimes come from disappointments.

- Learn five ways to be able to embrace positive or negative information about yourself from a neutral perspective, so necessary to see what you can't see.

Chapter 7: Clear Sight Principle 2—Imagine Positive Possibilities
The mind-set to hold in working with blind spots is not about eliminating weaknesses. It is a single-minded focus on connecting with a constant supply of energy, vitality, and resilience.

- Learn to use your imagination to stay flexible and open to opportunities.

Chapter 8: Clear Sight Principle 3—Simply Focus on Success
Blind spots may be standing in the way of your current goals for success.

- As you uncover blind spots, you may find that how you define success will also change.

Chapter 9: Clear Sight Principle 4—Stretch Your Strengths
Make turning blind spots into strengths enjoyable and easy, or else you'll lose momentum.

- Find out how to tap the strengths you already have to find ways to boost skills blocked by blind spots.

Chapter 10: Clear Sight Principle 5—Choose with Confidence
If you lack confidence and well-being in seeking a goal, determine whether you hold an inaccurate self-assessment or old emotional information. Either could be holding you back.

- Use the *Confidence Triangle* to be sure you think and feel the confidence you need to achieve your goal.

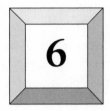

Shift to Neutral

When you're driving a car and believe you are lost, you can stop and shift to neutral gear to get your bearings for a moment. The same applies to considering blind spots. You need to halt momentarily and examine how and where you are going with your current habits. Do you want to keep operating exactly the same way or would you like to make a few alterations? *Shift to Neutral* is the first principle of clear sight. When we shift to neutral, we get the chance to see things about ourselves that we couldn't see before.

- We can be equally receptive to positive and negative feedback about ourselves, considering each for what information it brings us rather than how we are judged.
- We stop and reconsider how and why we act in certain ways.
- We are not captives of our feelings but are able to consider the reasons we feel the way we do.
- We are able to examine our motivations, motives, and mistakes without bias; we simply observe how they happen as if we are viewing a picture.
- We are able to make new choices.

In short, we become self-aware. Sometimes in the speed of the moment, we try to skip this step. An experience I had with a client of mine named Stephen reminded me of its fundamental importance.

A high-flying star in his early career, Stephen joined a new company as senior vice president of a manufacturing operation. The company culture reinforced a lot of group decision making and collegial relationships. He was used to operating independently and hierarchically. The new company conducted 360° feedback on its highest ranking 100 mangers. To Stephen's chagrin, his first 360° results revealed many negative perceptions from his boss, peers, and direct reports. In fact, out of his boss's 14 direct reports, Stephen scored last.

Shocked by the results, Stephen determined to turn them around. He followed the approach presented in this book, and worked conscientiously to recognize his blind spots and develop a Clear Sight Plan. When the following year's company 360° feedback came around, I hoped that Stephen would rank in the middle of his peers. However, Stephen ranked Number 1—not just overall but on almost every question.

Of course I believe in this work, but even I was surprised to see such dramatic results. No doubt Stephen's focus and hard work were most important to his success. However, I asked Stephen what we had done together that could have made a difference. Was it the assessment tools or the strategies? He thought very carefully, and then looked at me and said, "I know exactly what it was. You allowed me to see myself without judgment, and with that I was able to make conscious choices."

By "seeing myself without judgment," Stephen was referring to what I call the Shift to Neutral.

Developing New Habits

Shift to Neutral has been recognized by many successful and insightful people as absolutely essential to success. It is only in the neutral state that we gain the perspective to see ineffective habits in new ways.

As J. Paul Getty recognized: "The individual who wants to reach the top must appreciate the might of the force of habit—and must understand that practices are what create habits. He must be quick to break those habits that will break him—and hasten to adopt those practices that will become the habits that help him achieve the success he desires."

The Shift to Neutral occurs in that moment when we comprehend that we have habits that are not effective. It is often difficult for high-achieving people to allow themselves to see this information. Why? They see this as a sign of weakness or failure, and their competitive striving just will not allow them to admit their shortcomings even for a moment.

As Dan Goleman points out in *Working with Emotional Intelligence*, most of us share this propensity toward denial, as a way of protecting ourselves from disturbing feelings that come from acknowledging the truth about ourselves. Such defensiveness is evidenced as we minimize facts, rationalize, and filter information and anything else that prevents us from facing our own emotional truth.

It's no wonder that those who are able to able to embrace the truths about their strengths and limitations are distinguished in the workplace. In a 12-organization study of several hundred managers, the top performers were also the ones who were recognized for accuracy in self-assessment—a skill that the weakest performers lacked. Awareness of one's strengths and limitations helps top performers know where they should put their improvement effort and whom they should add to the teams they work with to supplement the strengths they lack.

What Holds Us Back

Sometimes a habit that we see as important to success is actually a disguised blind spot. For example, Henry prided himself on his compulsive hard work, which took precedence over family and everything else in his life. He drove others with the same intensity. As he took on larger assignments, his stress levels were upsetting everyone else including his boss. He was constantly distracted from what others were saying and appeared emotionally irritable in meetings. While the business results he produced were impressive, his lack of composure made those around him uncomfortable.

Henry's boss tried to explain this discomfort to Henry without success. Henry had held the habit of compulsiveness for so long that he assumed that constant high anxiety was a necessary state for success.

Totally out of touch with his own feelings about himself, Henry was also unaware of how his feelings were affecting others. He lacked emotional awareness. Yet since this was such a long-standing habit, the thought of changing it was overwhelming. In effect, Henry's sense of who he was included this feeling of compulsive anxiety. It was part of his unconscious personal portrait.

The idea of shifting to neutral was foreign to Henry. He was acting like the driver of a car who goes too fast until he comes to a red light, when he crashes on the brakes. When the light turns green, he floors the gas pedal and jumps to 60 miles per hour. Neutral may be a gear on the gear shift but not one he has ever consciously used.

People like Henry who live within the limitations of their blind spots never see the need to shift to neutral until they have a crash. They miss a promotion, get fired, or for the first time in their careers find themselves seriously stymied at work. Unfortunately, instead of shifting to neutral, they often move further into their own world of anxiety and unconstructive emotion. Never having experienced life without anxious feelings, they don't know any other way. Three examples of such losing emotional strategies for dealing with setbacks are sustained anger, blame, and withdrawal. They are further described in the chart on the next page.

Anger

Anger is a natural response to having one's dreams taken away. We can get angry at a boss, peer, or person who works for us when they disappoint us. For example, in Chapter 1 when Joey realized he wasn't given the sales management role, he became angry. He felt he was treated unfairly. He wanted to leave the company. While this behavior served as an emotional release, it would have been self-defeating if maintained for too long. Others would have simply been more convinced that Joey was not ready for a management role. Joey would have defeated himself by "*becoming anger*," meaning the emotion would have taken over control of his choices. He would no longer

Anger	Anger can be a natural immediate response to disappointment. When we hold it for too long, we are stuck in being that emotion and cannot gain a neutral perspective.
Blame	Blaming someone else for a disappointment may be entirely justified. However, if we hold on to the blame for too long, we don't take responsibility for the goal we set for ourselves.
Withdrawal	Withdrawal within oneself can provide a moment for recuperation. However, if we stay within ourselves too long, we don't become active in reaching our goals.

Strategies That Prevent Us from Shifting to Neutral

have been able to experience the freedom that comes from shifting to neutral and seeing fresh possibilities. Anger would have defined his personal self-portrait.

Blame

Others go a step beyond anger and place responsibility on other people for their own problem. Joey's initial feeling was that "management was a bunch of suits who didn't value top performance." He briefly questioned his boss's competency and blamed his peers for jealousy. This was another momentary reaction that helped Joey to deal with disappointment. If he had continued blaming others, he would have been seen as immature and irresponsible. He would have been locked into a blind spot that didn't allow him to see possibilities for getting others to support his becoming a manager.

Withdrawal

In Chapter 2 Emma, the newly named vice president of marketing, experienced a feeling of being overwhelmed by her new position and began to withdraw. Recognizing a lack of respect from several of those who reported to her, she experienced a loss of self-confidence and became extremely self-critical. In this state, she began to retreat into herself and back away from solving the problem. If she had continued this behavior, Emma would have reinforced feelings of those already questioning her ability. She would have "*become the feeling of retreat*," allowing the feeling of retreat to give her choices. In effect, she would have slowly lost control, and would not have been able to shift to neutral. Instead, Emma chose to leave these unconstructive feelings behind and was able to shift to neutral and find ways to regain a sense of confidence and authority.

Turning Points

A shift to neutral occurs the moment an individual stops, thinks, and makes a choice to either stay the course of current behavior or change direction. I have watched people make the shift as their eyes clearly are focused inside themselves while they process what they will do in the next moment. If the choice is to change, I often see a shift of expression and posture accompanied by a deepening and calm in their voices. *It is almost as if time has stopped and then started again.*

I remember the turning point for Joey's shift to neutral. He was criticizing his boss and everyone else in the organization for not recognizing his top performance. He ranted and raved about the unfairness. When there was a pause in the conversation, I looked at Joey and said quietly, "Joey you have a choice to make. We can sit together examining how unfairly you have been treated. I don't doubt that there was some unfairness in these events. Let's assume everything negative you say about everyone in your company is true and you are right; how does that help you to reach your goal?"

I continued, "The alternative is to look closely at your goal of becoming a sales manager, determine any blind spots you have that are getting in your way, and develop strategies for clear sight to overcome these obstacles. It's your choice. But you can choose only one of these alternatives."

Joey decided to put all his effort into the sales management goal. He consciously pushed feelings of anger and blame out of his mind, focusing only on those activities that would further his goal. In other words, he shifted to neutral. Committed to getting the next sales management position, Joey put his effort into identifying his blind spots. Any time negative feelings would start to emerge, he pictured himself sitting in the next sales manager's desk and took a deep breadth.

Emma Recommits to Herself

While Emma was withdrawing, she began to dwell on how her problem was linked to being one of the few women vice presidents in the company. She blamed some of the trouble she was having in her position on the highly patriarchal culture. These thoughts made her withdraw further and feel more negative about herself.

I had a conversation with Emma: "You have a choice to make. It's clear that you are dealing with a culture that historically has not placed women in senior roles. We can stay focused on the reasons why you feel women have been wronged in this company. Or you can put your efforts into demonstrating that a woman with your talent can be very effective in a vice presidential position. If you choose this second path, then you better direct your efforts toward figuring out what blind spots are preventing you from feeling fully confident in your job."

Emma chose to focus on being an effective female vice president. She began to problem solve to identify her blind spots and how she could move forward. Like Joey, she shifted her perspective to neutral.

Driving My Silver Gray Mercedes

Whenever I speak to a group of people about blind spots, I always introduce my silver gray sports Mercedes. It's a plastic model and only one foot long, but seeing it communicates a sense of what Shift to Neutral really means.

I originally heard the term Shift to Neutral from my high school driver's ed teacher. Neutral gear was designed for idling—motor on and ready to move in any direction. Whether I'm at a stop sign or sitting in a parking lot, I am ready to go forward or backward at a shift of my gear.

Neutral is when I can think about the power and beauty of the car. I love the smell of the leather interior. Not distracted by speed, nor having to stretch my neck to see what's behind me when I back up, I simply can idle for a few moments and enjoy this precision instrument.

As I start driving, I recognize the blind spots that may exist behind my shoulders, those places where I can't see an oncoming car through my rearview mirror. Occasionally I think I can save time just by looking in the side mirror. Why bother turning my head again? I've changed lanes a million times without any problem. Starting to cross the lane, I hear a horn and suddenly realize I missed the car in my blind spot. Thank goodness I didn't cause an accident.

Blind spots in relationships are much the same. Given the way we're engineered to think and feel, we simply have difficulty seeing how other people view us. Unless we make the effort to get their perspective, we may get caught in an unforeseen accident. By periodically Shifting to Neutral and checking perceptions, we maintain accident-free relationships.

The Art and Science of Emotional Awareness

While we were trained in school to analyze the stream of *thoughts* that come to mind all day, it is only recently that scientists and educators recognize the need to understand the constant flow of *feelings*. This *emotional information* includes the moment-to-moment meaning we understand from the experience of our feelings, physical body sensations, and emotional memories. In contrast to thoughts and ideas, which seem logical and principled, emotional information is personal and subjective and provides critical insights for our decisions.

Neuroscientist Antonio Damasio has explored the interrelationships between the rational and emotional components of the mind. As we sort out our thoughts, the mind also provides us emotional information in the form of a gut feeling or hunch that makes a decision feel right or wrong to us. While these gut feelings are fleeting, they are important signals about whether what we are doing fits into our preferences and beliefs about ourselves.

When we shift to neutral, we give ourselves the momentary opportunity to receive our gut feelings. Without the shift, we make ourselves vulnerable to overreacting to our steady stream of thoughts. We don't process the steady stream of feelings we experience and are in danger of emotional buildups of anger and withdrawal that can derail us.

Shifting to neutral lies at the heart of developing self-awareness, which is the essential skill for emotional competencies that distinguish star performers in today's workplace. Dan Goleman identifies three inter-related skills needed for self-awareness: (1) *emotional awareness*, knowing how our emotions affect our performance and having a sense of our inner values and goals; (2) *accurate self-assessment*, a sense of our strengths and weaknesses; and (3) *self-confidence*, the courage that comes from clear self-knowledge of our capability, values, and goals. These are the skills we both need and further develop as we recognize our blind spots and gain clear sight.

How to Shift to Neutral

A shift to neutral can involve a long period of contemplation where we get perspective on our feelings, values, career, and life. More frequently it involves a moment of breaking focus from what we are doing to process our immediate thoughts and emotional information.

Sounds simple, right? For many people, this one minute break seems impossible to fit into their busyness. I remember a conversation I had with another executive coach who shared how so many of her female clients were finding it impossible to take a bathroom break in a six-hour period due to their intense work commitments. This was a new blind spot I hadn't encountered before. However, it is a sad but true story of how we allow ourselves to lock into unconstructive habits.

Shifting our consciousness into neutral provides a space to decide whether the course of thought and action we are on is where we want to keep going. Or should we consider new possibilities and change directions? Let's consider five simple ways that we can shift to neutral in the course of our everyday work.

Get Your Goal in Perspective

An important career management approach is to regularly examine your goals to make sure you are clear about what you want and why. Self-awareness offers a guide to test whether what we are doing is in harmony with our dreams, hopes, feelings, and inner values. Reflection on a goal can put us immediately in touch with the need to shift a behavior or feeling we are having toward one that is more closely aligned with our goals.

Both Joey and Emma used a focus on their primary goal as an important way to move away from anger, blame, and retreat and to shift back to the neutral. Joey wanted his shot at a management job. Emma wanted to demonstrate that she could handle her expanded management assignment. Anytime the anger or desire to retreat would return, they would consciously move their attention back to the primary goal.

Reflect on Your Personal Model

Creating your personal model as we did in Chapter 4 is another important way to shift to neutral. As you reflect on your strengths, potential blind spots, and the meaning of success in your life, you provide yourself an opportunity to gain self-knowledge. You also have the chance to gauge what has changed in your inner feelings and thoughts since the previous time you set personal goals.

A model also provides a tool for discussing thoughts about yourself with someone else. When coaching someone, I find it helpful to converse about the model of the individual rather than talking to the individual about himself. With the model, we can engage in sharing observations collaboratively.

This style of communicating makes it easier for someone to talk about blind spots, which can be an anxiety-producing subject. It also helps the individual to see how he is seen through the eyes of others, and helps me to see the world through his eyes. This furthers our ability to develop effective strategies for clear sight.

Finally, the model provides a succinct summary of the information we discover for review and update in future career or goal planning sessions.

Get Balanced Feedback

In Chapter 5, we discussed how getting balanced feedback is a good way to gather information about your blind spots. It is also an excellent way to shift to neutral. Welcoming both positive and negative information about oneself communicates self-confidence to others. Asking for it expresses a sign of desire for self-awareness. A study of superior performers reveals that they want to hear how others perceive them and realize this as valuable information.

When you initiate a request for balanced feedback, do it in a way that shifts the conversation to neutral. If you say, "How did I do in giving my speech," you are asking for someone else's judgment about yourself. If instead you ask, "What were the three best things and the three things you'd change if I did that presentation again," you are shifting to neutral. The responder can talk about the audience, the speech material, or things you did. You provide space to talk about your own performance without making it personal. If you keep the conversation even-tempered, you give the responder the opportunity to supply data and observations like "your blue shirt is attractive in this light, but doesn't seem to be as dynamic under neon lights." Or they may observe "the middle of the presentation seemed not to get a lot of attention from this audience; you might want to make it a little more conversational next time." These are behaviors you can debate and modify.

Looking for balanced feedback sets up an open-ended conversation where you can accumulate many observations others have about you, without forcing them to become personally critical, a position most people find very uncomfortable.

Imagine Yourself as Someone Else

To stay in a neutral position while talking with someone else about yourself, imagine that the discussion is not focused on you but on another person sitting in the room. In this way, you can ask questions, use humor, and express appreciation for any negative comments. The comfort level of your response makes it easy for others to share negative views that can be helpful. The more enthusiasm you can express about receiving negative feedback, the more information you will receive. You also set the stage for future informal conversations.

When Joey held a meeting with his boss to find out why he hadn't gotten the sales management job, he still had a lot of pent-up anger. He used this technique of pretending the discussion was not focused on him but on someone else in the room. As the meeting went on, he actually began to believe he was talking about someone else. He spent a lot of time listening to gather information about his shortcoming for the management position.

Surprisingly, Joey found that as he got more information, he became less defensive. He just kept imagining that everyone was talking not about him, but about that "other person like him sitting in the room." As he slowly understood other people's perspective, he began to see a new view of himself that seemed logical and reasonable. His defensiveness seemed to evaporate.

Use Stress Management Techniques

There are many relaxation techniques for dealing with stress. Most of these will also be applicable for shifting to neutral. It is important to recognize when you are trapped in an emotion and need to find a way to return to a neutral space. Deep breathing and guided imagery are excellent techniques for staying neutral.

One of my clients named Louise, who had to face a difficult discussion with a sometimes emotionally abusive boss, developed one of her own techniques. She would easily withdraw when hit with too many negative comments. Sometimes she even felt the tears about to come. Feeling this moment coming on, she would imagine herself saying directly to her boss, "Kiss my _____." This thought would immediately drive her to the urge to laugh. The result was a shift to neutral, where she was in a far better position to engage in a constructive conversation with her boss.

Time for You to Shift to Neutral

Before leaving Chapter 6, identify a way you use to shift to neutral either alone or in conversations with others. Over the next week, make a note on your calendar committing yourself to creating at least two opportunities to shift to neutral. Make note of this in your personal self-portrait.

Having created the mental and emotional space to see new possibilities, you're ready to turn to Chapter 7 for the Second Principle of Clear Sight: Imagine Positive Possibilities.

Imagine Positive Possibilities

TO SEE WHAT WE CAN'T SEE is to imagine new possibilities. Imagining the possibilities we have within us to face and replace our blind spots is the mission of this book. The mindset I hold in working with blind spots is not about eliminating weaknesses. It is a single-minded focus on creating new ways to connect with a constant supply of energy, vitality, and resilience. We use our imaginations to stay flexible, buoyant, and open to new opportunities. *Imagine Positive Possibilities* is the second principle of clear sight.

Harvard professor Daniel Gilbert in his book *Stumbling on Happiness* says, "To imagine is to experience the world as it isn't and never has been, but as it might be." This according to Gilbert is the human brain's greatest achievement. It is the one thing no machine has been able to replicate. It also works to help us remember things in ways that provide a sense of normal reality. While the future may be very different from what our imagination portrays, we believe the pictures that our brain creates for us about the future's potential, and we find them motivational.

A particularly troublesome blind spot is one that limits our ability to use our imagination or to use it in only limiting ways.

- We choose to view things that happen to us only from a negative perspective.

- We view situations in rigid ways that make us unable to imagine alternative scenarios.
- We refuse to consider new activities that could bring us clear sight.

Freeing our imagination to see positive possibilities is so important because it is a tool we use to identify and release all our other blind spots. Also, when our imagination is constrained by blind spots, our motivation is significantly decreased.

Robert Allen, author of "Release the Brakes," points out that successful people know how to constantly change their limiting beliefs and self-images. Most people live in a *comfort zone*, an accumulation of beliefs formed from negative thoughts that we reinforce across a lifetime. These beliefs train us to limit ourselves to linear thinking about what we can't do. Successful people believe that they are never stuck because they are able to flood their thoughts and images with a new reality. They constantly adjust their self-image and behaviors to stay positive.

Unfortunately, Mason was one of those people who lived in a comfort zone of negative beliefs.

Mason Imagines the Worst

When I met Mason I realized he was successful by many measures. Unfortunately he was not a person who used his imagination in positive ways. His story has played out in many workplaces. He was a smart, capable individual who had been worn down by stress and pressure and had begun to expect the worst. He had not learned to shift to neutral and was vulnerable to seeing negative possibilities.

The manager of a large direct marketing operation in the Midwest, Mason had a strong track record of performance. He had recently been informed by his boss that people were complaining about some morale issues in Mason's operation that he wanted Mason to look into and resolve. The boss did not express particular concern and mentioned a number of other things that were going very well.

While Mason remained calm about the morale issue in the presence of his boss, he was agitated and furious at the thought of being criticized by people in his organization. He thought, "How could my boss doubt my competence? Something else must be going on I don't know about. I wonder if he's trying to build a case against me." Motivated by blind spots related to stress and perfection, Mason imagined the worst possible scenarios, became angrier, and withdrew from considering the matter further.

In reality Mason's boss saw the issue as something he hoped Mason would look into and resolve as a routine matter. By not taking any action, Mason was raising questions in the minds of others. His lack of movement was making his boss question whether there really was something more significant going on. Did the morale issues indicate a deeper problem that no one had noticed before? The more Mason hunkered down, the more his resistance stimulated the imagination of others to believe something was really wrong.

What was happening to Mason's outlook is a process Daniel Gilbert calls "filling-in." When the mind forecasts something in the future, it will fill in the details to make the future picture reasonable and complete. In effect, Mason was filling-in facts that completed his doomsday scenario, while others around him were filling-in a future prediction based on their observations of his inaction. Of course both scenarios were based on slim concrete fact. But in stressful environments where cutbacks and layoffs are a way of life, our imaginations are easily triggered to expect negative outcomes.

The real source of the morale problem was related to how Mason handled his stress by getting rigid and overly demanding. The solution, which we discuss in Chapter 13, was relatively simple. He needed to relax and be more flexible in handling problems with his staff.

But the situation was escalating to something much larger because of Mason's inaction. Motivated by embarrassment and discomfort, his active imagination was creating a picture of his boss trying to force him out of the organization, and his boss was reacting by imagining a much larger issue going on. An imagination shift was called for.

Shifting His Imagination

Mason reluctantly asked me to work with him to try to find a way to handle this problem. He was feeling defeated and unable to generate any energy. While the focus was the morale issue, I noticed that he seemed to be fatigued and unable to handle the constant pressure of his operation. He also was disappointed that his boss would criticize him.

We went through a series of decisions together. Did he really want to stay in his job? Yes. Did he think sitting in his office doing nothing about the morale issue was in his best interests of keeping his job? No. Did he think his boss would be impressed by his doing nothing about the morale issue? No. Would it be worth getting information about the morale issue so he would know what it was about? Probably.

This was a way of moving from the negative imagining back to reality, task, and action. Mason slowly relaxed and began to let go of his extreme negative fantasies. He re-engaged in the work he knew how to do best—solve problems. We set up a plan to gather information from some of his people and define what the real issue was all about.

Once Mason had re-engaged and had admitted that there could be possible positive outcomes to his predicament, he was able to take some positive steps. He practiced shifting to neutral. He asked each member of his team to help him to focus on his own development plan. He gathered some more information about what might be causing the complaints. The more confident he felt, the more assertive he became in managing the effort in a positive way. Mason ultimately filled his boss in on what was going on related to the morale issue.

By shifting to neutral and then imagining the potential for positive outcomes, Mason was able to manage a constructive course of action. The problem that he imagined could alter his career became manageable.

While this story may seem hard to believe when looked at objectively, it is one that plays out in many businesses these days. People are working hard, pushing for results, handling too much activity, and struggling for balance. Under these conditions, our imaginations can lead us to fill in gloomy scenarios. We talk about how to manage the underlying stress that creates the catalyst for such negative thoughts in Chapter 13.

The moral of the Mason story is to make sure to use your imagination in constructive ways.

How Pessimism Becomes Optimistic

As we've seen with Mason, imagination can create limitations. Dr. Martin Seligman has researched the way we learn to explain to ourselves why things happen. The optimist feels the energy to take control over things, while the pessimist may feel a sense of helplessness. We perform less effectively when we see ourselves as more limited in affecting future events. While pessimism may be an appropriate stance for observing certain business situations, it works against our motivation to try new things. So how can pessimistic thinking be turned a bit in the optimistic direction? My work with Joshua exemplified this important transition.

Joshua Reevaluates His Career

Joshua, age 35, had come to a time in his career when he felt the need to reevaluate the potential for his career. He had a solid history of job experience in the accounting profession and had held a series of positions for accounting firms and Fortune 500 companies. However, he felt his career had stalled and wanted my help to take a fresh look at his future potential.

As I got to know Joshua, I realized he was one of those people who has the potential to be a *level 5 leader*, as defined by Jim Collins in his breakthrough book *Good to Great*. These leaders are people who combine what Collins calls *professional will* with *personal humility*. In other words they create results, set standards for the long run, and take responsibility for poor performance while at the same time acting with quiet determination, channeling ambition into the company and giving credit to others, not themselves.

Joshua had the will, but perhaps a bit too much humility. When I asked him to describe the strengths he brought to his job, he spoke about doing the job to expected results without fanfare and applause. He had a good track record of producing results and had the experience and credentials to move ahead. Yet Joshua was just not connected to the energy and optimism that would help him see positive possibilities *for himself.*

As we began to discuss his situation, I asked Joshua to list the greatest strengths that he brings to his position. He listed these:

- Follow-through to results.
- Decision making.
- Analytic skills.
- One-on-one communication.
- Empathy for his team.
- Resilience.
- Humor.

As I looked and listened to his list, I thought it sounded like a solid set of skills, well-adapted to a managerial position in his profession. However, when Joshua talked abut these skills, he described them as "kind of average," nothing to get excited about, abilities that "everybody has." His perspective went beyond humility to borderline self-deprecation. For example, when I asked him about how he felt about these qualities in himself, he said, "Follow-through to results describes somebody boring, sort of a Boy Scout type who just always gets the job done as asked." He described his empathy for his team as his "being a pushover, not a leader." And his analytical skills were felt as "a mad scientist, weird with not very good communication skills."

Joshua had a big blind spot. He was more than pessimistic. He was not emotionally connecting to his own strengths. Rather than feeling the energy that comes from knowing he does something well, Joshua was observing his skills and explaining how unimportant they were in the scheme of things. Somewhere earlier in his life, Joshua had learned to judge himself against standards that constantly made him feel less than okay. This pattern of disconnect was an old habit for Joshua, which we explore further in Chapter 12.

Create Positive Possibilities Using Imagination

To help Joshua to see more positive possibilities for himself, I asked him to use his imagination to describe how he would feel about these same skills in someone else whom he wanted to work for. Immediately the emotion he felt attached to each skill began to change:

- Follow-through—"I respect this person. This is someone who takes pride in their work and is concerned about others."
- One-on–one communication—"This is someone I want to work for. I bet he is a great coach and motivator."
- Empathy for his team—"This person is interested in the whole team succeeding, not just in his own pursuits."

After doing this exercise, Joshua went back a second time to identify his feelings about *his own* skills and was far better able to imagine the positive possibilities:

- "My follow-through results in the ability to get things done."
- "My empathy suggests an excellent coach and motivator in one-on-one situations."
- "Decision making for results suggests someone who doesn't waste time, someone who keeps things moving."

For each of the initial skills named, Joshua was able to see positive possibilities that made him *feel* stronger. He was beginning to let go of seeing himself as limited and not desirable to recognizing that he really had a lot to offer. He had used his imagination to create positive possibilities for himself.

Resilience

Richard Davidson, who studied the difference between resilient and nonresilient people at the University of Wisconsin, noted that the resilient people handle stress differently. They use their optimism to put solutions into action. When something is wrong, they start to think about how to solve the problem.

This is fundamental to recognizing and changing our blind spots. If we are to see the possibilities for turning blind spots into strengths rather than weaknesses, we must choose optimism. We need to be able to shift to neutral in times of negativity and stress and use our imagination to foresee new alternatives for ourselves. That is why developing our imaginative abilities for positive thinking is one of the key principles for maintaining clear sight.

Now it's your turn to imagine at least one possibility for yourself that could apply to any area of your life, whether it be work, relationships, fun, or serious time. Let it be a possibility that lets you feel joy and a positive sense of who you are. Savor it for a moment! Record it in your personal self-portrait.

With your mind ready to imagine positive possibilities, you are ready for the third principle of clear sight: Simply Focus on Success.

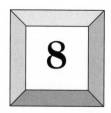

Simply Focus on Success

SUCCESS HAS DIFFERENT meanings for each individual. Some look for power and control. Others seek meaningful relationships. The ability to balance work with our lives is becoming important to many. We can view success from the short-term perspective of a project or assignment, or the long-term perspective of a career or life choice. Whatever you choose as your goal, your ability to state that goal clearly will influence your success in reaching it. The third principle of clear sight focuses on goal clarity so you can *Simply Focus on Success*. We view our blind spots within the context of the goal we choose to reach.

Regardless of how you define success, recognizing relevant blind spots will influence how effectively you reach your goals. It may also change the focus of the goals you set for yourself in the future. For example:

- Different goals will lead us to deal with different blind spots.
- Some blind spots may be rooted in long-standing habits and may affect our career goals.
- Other blind spots may be more situational in nature and occur only in relationship to particular settings, people, or short-term goals.
- Understanding blind spots increases knowledge about our strengths, weaknesses, wants, and desires and may change the nature of our future goals.

- This increased self-knowledge may also lead us to changing our understanding of what success means to us.

In short, understanding our blind spots influences not only whether we meet our goals but also the very nature of the goals we set for ourselves.

Why People Work

There are widely different purposes for people coming to work. According to social scientists, around one-third of Americans see financial reward, rather than the nature of the work, as the primary purpose of their work. In a 2006 MetLife Employee Benefits Trend Study, 58 percent of all employees reported that their top consideration when joining an employer is the quality of co-worker and customer relationships. Young Baby Boomers 41 to 50 (61%) and preretirees 61 to 69 (67%) cite relationships as the deciding factor. More than half (56% of men and 58% of women) cite work/life balance as the key job criterion.

According to the U.S. Department of Labor, the top reason people leave their jobs is due to lack of appreciation. The boss relationship is particularly important. In one study of healthcare workers, it was found that when people worked for a boss they disliked, their blood pressure rose significantly, increasing the risk of heart disease by 16 percent and stroke by 33 percent.

People work for a variety of reasons. What makes them feel successful? The Dalai Lama in his book *The Art of Happiness at Work* emphasizes the link between one's underlying attitude and one's sense of satisfaction with his work. Psychologist and NYU business professor Dr. Amy Wrzesniewski conducted a 1997 study that explored how life and work satisfaction is more dependent on how employees see their work than on income or status. The study revealed how workers generally fall into three categories of perspectives toward work.

- The first group sees work as a way of earning money. The nature of the work is unimportant. They will change jobs and adjust their way of doing things to earn more money.

- The second group understands work in terms of a career. They will be motivated by the status, promotions, power, and prestige that come with advancement. When advancement stops, they will change positions. Work requires a greater personal investment for this group than the first group.
- The third group views their work as a calling. There is less separation between the work and personal lives of these people. They see the meaningfulness of their work, and would do this work if they could afford it without getting paid. They have the highest work and life satisfaction of any of the three groups.

What's the Meaning of Success?

In 1996 and 2001, 140 Harvard MBA graduates were asked how they defined success. Most important was personal satisfaction or "balance," then the respect of peers, followed by a CEO or CFO role. High salaries ranked last.

Certainly the quest for power is still alive and well. But the trade-off of time for money is increasingly important. Having the time to give pleasure to family and friends is important. A reality of contemporary life is that we have so many options of things we want to do, but limited time to do them. Making decisions about how to spend our time is important.

When Inc. magazine gathered five entrepreneurs to define what The Good Life meant to them their answers reflected a number of trade-offs. One man said, "I've focused on freedom and balance. Balance is elusive when you start a business. . . . As for freedom—If you have a castle but you can't relax in it, that's not freedom."

Another person expressed the individual meaning of success: "It's subjective, and I celebrate that because what rocks in my world doesn't rock in another's. It's critical that everyone define success on their own terms."

What is clear is that the meaning of success is being reexamined by people of all ages and life stages. The trade-offs of time, personal satisfaction, giving pleasure to friends and loved ones, and having the freedom to do things you love are all part of the success equation.

Clearly the meaning of success for each of these groups is different. Think carefully about your own meaning of success and how you will define your goals in the coming months or year.

What is your goal for success? Whatever you are considering, make sure your goal statement is simple and clear. Malcolm Gladwell points out that the best decisions are made when we have boiled the issues down to a simple pattern of information. Too many facts can overload a decision maker. To reinforce his point he shares research done by Sheena Iyengar, who set up two tasting booths for jam at a grocery store. While common wisdom would suggest that consumers prefer more choices, Sheena found that consumers bought more jam from a display of 6 choices than from a display of 12 choices. Additional information creates too much distraction.

I believe the same underlying premise is true in setting up a framework for your goals. You need a simple, straightforward goal statement and strategy. The following three examples demonstrate how people define changing goals for success within their existing work. Blind spots will play an integral role in shaping and achieving their goals.

Success Goal #1: Seek Status, Promotion, and Money

Long-term success for Tony meant being promoted to chief financial officer with power, status, and financial rewards. Recognized as someone with potential within his company, Tony at 31 was a financial analyst seeking a management position. I met him early in his career as he was clarifying his career goals.

Tony began to identify any potential blind spots that could derail him by using the Blind Spots Profile, which verified what he thought he already knew about himself. He couldn't see how these potential blinds spots could interfere with his goal. He would quickly find out how short-sighted he really was. Following are his goals for success and the results of his Blind Spots Profile.

Tony: Financial Analyst, Age 31

Goal for Success: Long term: To become a CFO.

Short term: To become a manager.

Blind Spots Profile: Reserved Analytical Strategist.

Greatest Strength: Insightful, analytical ability to see both the forest and the trees.

Potential Blind Spot: Can be too much in his head and become distant/aloof from people.

I suggested Tony also take the Blind Spots 360, which indicated that he didn't read people well. I recognized that Tony was a strong, hard-driving, results-oriented analyst. His blind spot related to his lack of awareness of people's unstated desires, usually communicated through nonverbal cues. Tony didn't consider this a shortcoming. He believed that practical, objective people usually go into finance. They didn't need to be nonverbally sensitive.

Tony discovered how his blind spot could interfere with his goal in an unfortunate way. When he was assigned to develop financial projections about purchasing a new subsidiary, the division president kept returning his work with a request for more analysis. Tony got frustrated because he knew his analysis was complete, and complained that the division president was a moron. In fact, the president had unstated reasons for the purchase that were not financial, which Tony didn't try to understand.

Tony's blind spot was doing him in. His perspective was too narrow to read subtle cues about the president's intent. He was frustrating the president because he never asked the right questions. Shortly, the project was assigned to a new analyst, who was able to pose the right questions in a broader perspective. It was only when Tony was suddenly requested off the project that his boss recognized and explained to him what was happening.

Suddenly convinced that eliminating his blind spot was very important to his future success, Tony set a new success goal and Clear Sight Plan, identified next.

Tony's New Goal and Clear Sight Plan

Goal: Develop the ability to better understand the unexpressed, nonverbally communicated, nonfinancial needs of people.

Clear Sight Plan: Use well-developed analytical skills to identify questions to get nonfinancial info about others.

As he worked on this plan, Tony's people-reading ability and his clear sight for his career goals began to improve. I tell you more about how in the next chapter.

The next story of Grace reveals an apparently successful woman who finds the need to change her success goals as she discovers her blind spots.

Success Goal #2: Seek Energy and Balance

Grace's success goals had always been oriented toward promotion and expanded responsibility. She was achieving the type of power and promotional opportunities that Tony desired. Everyone viewed her as successful. At 38, she was running a major operating division. She had been promoted three times in the past five years. All feedback about her performance from her boss was terrific. The people who reported to her liked and respected her. What people saw from the outside was a manager highly successful in her work. Why would she need to look for blind spots?

Grace's personal experience of her work was quite different. She felt constantly tired, worn down, and was losing sleep. She felt overwhelmed by conflicts she had to resolve every day: staff members who didn't get along with one another; project team members who wanted her to settle logjams; peers who slowed down progress. She was dreading going to work. As Grace explained it, "Success to me means not only getting promotions and status, but also feeling a sense of personal well-being and enthusiasm for what I am doing. While no one around me has a clue, I have grown to hate my work and am thinking of changing careers."

As Grace reexamined her career goals, she set a new success goal for herself: *Find ways to achieve a better balance between the demands of the job and the energy and balance I feel in myself.* She also completed the Blind Spots Profile and Blind Spots 360 and found a blind spot that was affecting her wear and tear on the job, as you can see in the following results.

Grace: Division Manager, Age 38

Goal for Success: Personal well-being and energy.

Blind Spots Profile: Warm Relationship Builder.

> Greatest Strength: Innate understanding of other's needs/feelings.

> Potential Blind Spot: Avoid negative feelings from others.

Feedback from Blind Spots 360: Normally upbeat, Grace is getting bossy.

As her results point out, Grace's strength was her warmth and ability to create harmony in groups of people. It came naturally to her, but her empathy was being overstretched and she was becoming bossy. Her blind spot resulted from trying to avoid negative feelings. She preferred to use kind words and encourage people to get along. As the scope of her job increased she needed to get more efficient in handling negative feelings and feedback. With her new goal for success, she also set the new Clear Sight Plan that follows.

Clear Sight Plan: Set boundaries and transfer responsibility to others; let others resolve their own conflicts; learn stress management techniques.

Grace explained the reasoning behind the plan: "As the work multiplied, I needed to learn to push back on others to resolve their own problems. I was not seeing how I was absorbing all my own and everybody else's stress. I needed to be clearer with others about my expectations for their doing things in ways less stressful for me." By implementing her new Clear Sight Plan, Grace was able to achieve her goal of increasing her energy and sense of balance without changing careers.

The third story of Neil shows how someone can find success through new dimensions for personal growth within the scope of their existing job.

Success Goal #3: Work Effectively with Difficult Individuals

Increasingly we work with and through other people. You may like to work alone, but the minute you have to sell a product, persuade others about your position, or manage a project, you probably will find at least one individual who is difficult to work with.

> Consider Neil, a 40-year-old middle school history teacher. He was recognized as a master teacher and had the respect of parents, students, and other teachers. He had achieved most of the goals he had set out for himself as a teacher and wanted to find some new challenges to energize his teaching. He noticed how some kids "pushed his buttons" and sometimes made him lose his temper. This seemed like a challenge worth looking into and Neil set a new success goal to find a more effective way to deal with these difficult students.

Neil took the Blind Spots Profile to see what might be causing his difficulty. The results are summarized below.

Neil: Teacher, Age 40

Goal for Success: Learn to work more effectively with students who "push his buttons."

Blind Spots Profile: Responsible High-Standards Builder

> Greatest Strength: Innate self-discipline for doing things the right way.

> Potential Blind Spot: Can become too serious, distant, angry, and inflexible.

Feedback from Others: Tough teacher; high standards; sometimes too demanding.

To understand his blind spots, Neil began to think about his greatest strength: "I persevere to see that things are done the right way. My classroom has rules. I expect students to respect those rules and create an environment where we all want to work." What does his strength look like when overused? "I guess I can get overcontrolling."

Neil further observed that the kinds of students who "pushed his buttons" were the ones who were most resistant to authority and rules, as well as those who were perfectionists. In other words, these were the kids who were opposite to him or most like him. Neil's blind spot is one that I call *Old Habits*, ways of thinking and acting that have become fixed over time. Since childhood, Neil had acted as the defender of the "right way" of doing things. The rebellious students he found difficult would probably irritate most other teachers, but they had an even stronger effect on Neil because they challenged his "right way." At the other extreme, kids who pushed his standards even higher made him feel judged and inadequate, so he held them to an unrealistic standard—similar to the way he treated himself.

Neil further refined his goal for success by developing his Clear Sight Plan:

Clear Sight Plan: Be aware of students similar to him or opposite to him in temperament and focus on staying flexible in understanding their perspective.

To achieve his plan's goal, Neil would identify those students who were most like or different from him, and be particularly attentive to them. He believed he would find more flexible ways to communicate with them if he took the time to get their perspective. He might even set a contract with these students to jointly work on such a plan.

By taking a fresh look at personal development goals within his existing job, Neil was able to find new challenges and growth for himself.

Now It's Your Turn

What is your goal for success? It's important to always be clear on your goal statement if you are going to eliminate blind spots that interfere.

Make a note of your current goal so you can think about it in the coming chapters. Record it in your personal self-portrait.

If you are having trouble deciding your success goal at this moment, choose one of the following seven items:

1. Visualize the wellness of the financial area of your life.
2. Consider your ideal job or career.
3. Contemplate the balance of your work/personal life.
4. Visualize your health and how it affects your life.
5. Consider your relationships.
6. Think about your personal growth needs.
7. Focus on your role in the community.

Any of these items may define an arena for your success goals. Set one goal for yourself. If you have more than one goal, determine the one most important to you at this time. Keep that goal in mind as we turn to "stretching your strengths" to accomplish it in Chapter 9.

9

Stretch Your Strengths

In developing your clear sight strategy, always start from your greatest strength. It provides you with a quick read of the primary skill you can rely on to help develop areas that need attention. Thinking about your strengths helps you to develop a positive attitude where you more easily shift to neutral. In short, you gain perspective on the most constructive way to reach for success. *Stretch Your Strengths* is the fourth principle of clear sight.

Some important things to keep in mind about your strengths include:

- You can use your strengths to help develop your weaker skills and those associated with blind spots.
- The situation you are in influences how your strengths are perceived.
- Under stress you may begin to think of strengths and weaknesses as constant and inflexible.
- Your areas of gut strength may have potential for further development of intuitive abilities.

Distinguished performers are always open to opportunity. They actively seek out information about any ineffective habits. They welcome information about where their blind spots may be hiding. They consciously shift to neutral, because they know that only in that state can they gain

97

The Wisdom of Oprah's Spanx

Oprah Winfrey, who has spent much time helping her readers to look and feel their best, regularly praises the opportunities created by her Spanx. Offered in as many product variations as there are different types of bodies, a Spanx attempts to flatten those areas that are a little too well-endowed and build those areas that could use a little fluffing up. Stretching your strength is like using a Spanx. You borrow a little from an overused skill and use it to strengthen an underdeveloped skill.

If you're a strong analytical person, for example, but tend to be reserved in social situation, use your analytical skills to devise unique questions you can ask at the next company cocktail party to engage people in conversation. If you're seen as being too responsible and lacking innovative ideas, think about being responsible to yourself for having a good time at work. Then think up five things you'd like to do to make work joyful for you, and assume responsibility for making that happen.

Figure out a creative way to make blind spots fade by relying on one of your strengths. If you need help, invite a group to a Spanx Blind Spots Party, where each person gets to state a strength and blind spot. The Spanx approach to stretching your strengths has three requirements: Make it fun. Try something you've never done before. Laugh a lot when people recognize "how you've changed!"

---

the self-awareness they need to constantly balance their strengths for peak performance.

By *stretching our strengths*, we can use them to develop the vulnerabilities that our blind spots have created. Let's look at two examples demonstrating how this process actually works.

Tony Stretches to Understand People Needs

Remember Tony from Chapter 7? He was the 31-year-old analyst who defined his long-term goal to become a CFO, but first had to become an effective manager. Tony realized how blind he had been in assuming that his division president was unable to recognize the brilliance of his financial projections. Indeed, it was his own limitation that prevented him from seeing that the division president simply had nonfinancial requirements that Tony didn't understand. How chagrined Tony felt when his boss had to point out Tony's inability. He simply hadn't read the division president's feelings soon enough.

However, just because people-reading isn't a natural skill for Tony doesn't mean that he can't develop a high level of expertise in understanding other people's feelings. He needs to stretch his strength to use his insightful analytical skills to gather info about people's feelings. Unfortunately, when the mishap with the division president occurred, Tony believed he had a permanent handicap. Over a period of a few months he began to get proficient at understanding emotional needs by using his mental discipline to ask the right questions. He put the effort into making several checklists that he would use to be sure to uncover feelings or additional concerns. In fact, over time this attentiveness may help Tony to develop a more natural pattern recognition ability for identifying feelings and emotional needs.

Abigail also needs to stretch her existing strengths as a "motivating implementer" to develop the confrontational communication style that sometimes disempowers people.

Abigail Stretches to Communicate More Effectively

Abigail has always been three steps ahead of everyone else in understanding how to develop a new venture. With an Assertive-Get-It-Doner Blind Spots Profile (see Appendix), she knows how to get things done fast and has that instinctive ability to recognize the natural capacity of different individuals to implement her plan. She also has the extroverted energy to motivate others to share her vision. However, when she overuses her strengths, she can push too hard, too fast and disempower others.

Abigail's Blind Spots 360° feedback captured her blind spot. While she motivates others, she also can confuse them. When she moves too fast to implement a plan in her head, she can leave others behind. Then she gets frustrated with their lack of understanding, and begins to confront them about their shortcomings, which leads to trampling their feelings. They end up feeling abused and afraid to interact with her.

Of course, the blind spot actually resides with Abigail. She is blind to the fact that others cannot see the plan in her head unless she communicates it to them. In addition, her natural confrontational style can put people off, and make them feel intimidated. She needs to recognize that when people appear to be resistant or retreating, she needs to shift to neutral and reconsider how to motivate them—a natural strength of hers. Verbally attacking them only causes them to retreat further.

Abigail is stretching her gut-thinking from Think Instincts First to Think Thoughts First as is described in Chapter 4. By thinking thoughts first she looks for boundaries and structures that can help her to explain to others her vision and way of getting things done. While she still is not easily tuned into the feelings of other people, she has trained herself to stop and think about early warning signs of who she might be disenfranchising with her natural confrontational style. When she shifts to neutral, she recognizes the need to soften her communication. As a result Abigail is meeting less resistance to her plans and making more people comfortable with her leadership.

We can stretch our existing strengths as Abigail has done to turn existing weaknesses into new strengths. In addition, we can stretch our gut strengths to develop greater intuitive abilities of our existing strengths.

Stretch Your Gut Strengths

The quick thinking and feeling styles that form the Blind Spots Profile models help us to recognize how we think from the gut as part of our everyday decisions. These styles are part of an intuitive approach to decision-making. The strengths of each of the nine Blind Spots Profile models introduced in Chapter 4 are essentially a pattern recognition ability that forms the basis of our gut strength. While the question is still open to research, general belief in the field of psychology is that these perception styles are probably developed through a mix of genetics and life experiences.

In a study of 60 successful entrepreneurs whose companies have revenues from $2 million to $400 million, all reported using their intuitive, gut strengths in decision-making. Some used them at the outset while others said they helped to confirm their in-depth analysis. One said that after a systematic analysis he used his intuition to make a final decision.

Gut Strength and Intuition

Are gut strength and intuition the same thing? Perhaps. Sometimes the terms are used interchangeably. For clarity I refer to intuition as a more developed sense of gut strength, particularly for pattern recognition skills that seem to go beyond the gut strengths that we generally use in everyday life.

Neuropsychiatrist Shafica Karagulla spent eight years researching and discovering people such as newspaper reporters, doctors, businesswomen, and government leaders, who were able to obtain information in somewhat unexplainable ways. For example, doctors she interviewed were able to intuitively *see* a picture of a patient's internal organs and understand the type and location of illness.

All of the highly intuitive people Karagulla studied continued to rely on their professional approaches to problem solving. The doctors would run their tests and compare them to the inner vision they saw of a patient's illness. Businesspeople would run forecasts and see if the results matched the guidance they were receiving through other forms of perceptions. Dr. Karagulla reinforced the need for integrating information from all our senses if we are to make the best quality decisions.

While these types of experiences are still somewhat unique, I meet clients who are trying to understand strengths in pattern recognition that give them greater intuitive skills in problem solving. The more they develop these skills, the more they become aware of other reliable intuitive abilities.

Marcia Experiences a Sense of Being Different

Marcia was an advertising executive for a large national television advertiser. I met her when she was trying to better understand the power and stress of her intuitive abilities. She had been recognized as creative all her life and had gut strength in recognizing how people feel almost instantaneously. Her ad campaigns reflected her skills, and she was recognized throughout her profession as very capable, but perhaps a little unusual.

I worked with Marcia when she was feeling burned out by her job. While she had won awards for her advertising and had recently been promoted at her company, she was feeling tired and low in energy. She also had a strange sense of being different that she really couldn't explain very well. She completed the Blind Spots Profile and Blind Spot 360 to provide some initial information for our discussion. The results are summarized next.

Marcia: Advertising Executive, Age 41

Goal for Success: To understand her feelings of burnout and feeling different.

Blind Spots Profile: Sensitive Perceptive Creator.

> Greatest Strength: Perceive unique, creative ways of understanding the emotional needs of others.

> Potential Blind Spot: Can become too emotionally focused and ignore social expectations. Can overwork and become ill.

Feedback from Blind Spots 360: Sometimes her ideas are difficult to understand. She seems remote. She is highly creative.

As Marcia analyzed her major strengths, she realized for the first time that her intuitive ability to read feelings led her to take on the feelings of everyone around her. She literally would experience all the positive and negative feelings of those involved whenever she entered a room. Marcia's blind spot was in not realizing how to turn off her feeling perceptions. She had never realized that this experience was not one others shared. She developed the Clear Sight Plan identified next.

Clear Sight Plan: Create clear boundaries to not overextend my sensitive emotional system. Be clear with people on the responsibilities I expect them to carry.

As she attempted to gain clear sight, Marcia learned to set boundaries to insulate herself from carrying the emotional burdens of others. She had already suffered pneumonia two years ago and was in a state of burnout. If she didn't take these steps, she was going to become more ill. Marcia stretched her strengths by responding to her own feelings with the same level of responsibility she had always done with other people.

Marcia Begins to Understand Her Unique Skills

Marcia shared many of the qualities that Elaine Aron describes in her book *The Highly Sensitive Person*. These individuals are particularly aware of the sensory stimulation in their environment, and can become overly aroused. Especially perceptive, they have a deep understanding of ways to resolve conflicts and create group harmony through creative means.

Marcia processes an enormous amount of sensory input that she stores in her emotional brain for pattern recognition. I was not surprised when she began to discuss with me her questions about the intuitive feelings she was increasingly aware of. She couldn't explain how she knew certain things about the future that she had no way of knowing. She felt embarrassed to share these experiences with business colleagues because she thought others would see her as strange.

To better understand her experiences, Marcia went to a program offered by Dr. Henry Reed at Atlantic University in Virginia Beach. There she was able to work with others in supervised exercises related to different forms of perception. She would get instant feedback on the accuracy of her intuitive reactions. Most importantly, she was able to learn to comfortably integrate these tools with more traditional methods of information gathering and decision making. As a result, Marcia began to feel personally empowered rather than strange. She learned to talk about these experiences carefully, but only with people who would be sensitive and open-minded.

An Integrated Mind-Set

Researchers are only beginning to comprehend the subtle workings of our minds. The basic pattern recognition skills presented in our personal models are skills I have observed in hundreds of clients over the past 15 years. Other forms of perception similar to those experienced by Marcia are also coming to my attention in client discussions. The best guidance I can give to those who are experiencing similar skills is to engage in instruction that will help you to understand the potential and limitations of these abilities. In this way, you may better incorporate them into the integrated workings of your mind.

Before leaving this chapter, identify a strength of yours that can be stretched to accomplish your goals. Get a clear idea of how you can use it and for what purpose. Make this information part of your personal self-portrait. Then move on to Chapter 10 to understand the role that confidence plays in the principles of clear sight.

Choose with Confidence

SELF-CONFIDENCE IS a belief that we can achieve goals we set for ourselves. It comes from both knowing that we have the necessary skills and abilities, and a feeling of self-belief to be able to do what we plan. Self-confident people are willing to take risks. Even with failure these people have the resilience to keep believing in themselves. *Choose with Confidence* is the fifth and final principle of clear sight.

Most people have more confidence about themselves in certain situations than in others. For example they may feel confident about their technical abilities, but less confident about their skills to converse with new people. If one doesn't have much experience in conversing with new people, then the lack of confidence is probably appropriate. As we gain the skills and experience, our confidence should increase.

Confidence creates a blind spot when we retreat from goals that we are well prepared to accomplish or take on goals we are ill-prepared to reach. This could happen for several reasons:

- We have an exaggerated assessment of the value of our skills and abilities for the task.
- We have an undervalued assessment of our skills and abilities for the job.

- We have old feelings connected to the task, emotional information that defeats our belief in ourselves.
- We have old feelings connected to the task that influence us to take unnecessary risks.

Coach Mike Krzyzewski of Duke University's top-ranked basketball team sees confidence as an effective weapon against fear. In competition, he tells his players to never let their opponents see them down or worried. When others know they're getting to you, it gives them more confidence. You must have the expression of confidence on your face to win.

We can give signals that make us look confident. Even better, we can actually find ways to adjust our thoughts and feelings to increase our sense of confidence from within. The Confidence Triangle pictured here portrays the relationship among accurate assessment of skills, current emotional information, and confidence.

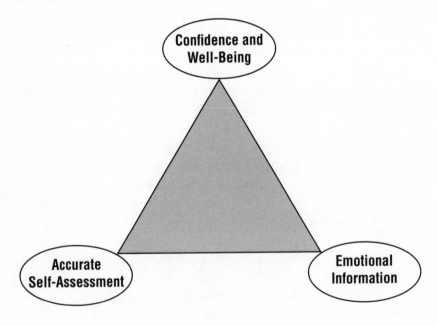

The Confidence Triangle

We are confident when we have an accurate self-assessment of our strengths and weaknesses *and* the feelings, which make up our emotional information, communicate a gut belief in that assessment. Our sense of confidence decreases when either our self-assessment *or* our emotional information communicates that something is missing. In short, confidence comes from a gut belief in our genuine skills.

We can adjust our confidence level by updating either our skill assessment or our emotional information. Let's observe how this works as Sean, who experienced a lack of confidence, sought a new career opportunity.

Sean Conducts a Job Search

Sean, age 40, was a vice president and head of investment planning for a company that merged with another. Feeling that his position and future career possibilities were uncertain, Sean wanted to pursue new opportunities for himself. He had changed jobs several times, through the efforts of a recruiter, but believed he needed to take some steps on his own. He asked me to help him organize his search process and we talked about his building a network. He developed a list of people to start contacting. We agreed to touch base in a couple of weeks to discuss his progress and any difficulties he was having.

Two weeks went by and Sean called to report no action; however, the alibis were starting to emerge. "I couldn't call because I had too much work. My daughter was sick. My wife was doing income tax." Fearing Sean might be stuck in a blind spot, I asked him to e-mail me every day with a simple statement of what he had or had not done, noting how he was *feeling* about it. I believed this emotional information might help Sean understand any blind spots limiting his progress. Eight days went by with Sean reporting no action, and then suddenly each day he made a call to a potential contact. As he confided, "I had to sink to the bottom of the barrel before I could move forward. Checking in with you, I realized there was only one way to go—up."

Sean had been stopped by the outdated feelings he sensed every time he started to conduct job seeking activities. The messages associated with these feelings were, "You're not good enough. No one will give you a new job. Forget it."

This emotional information was attached to old memories, but the job search activities seemed to stir them up. In short, his head was in one place and his feelings in another. Sean needed to update his reservoir of emotional information with new messages appropriate to the person he is today.

Sean and I talked through what was going on through a discussion of the Confidence Triangle.

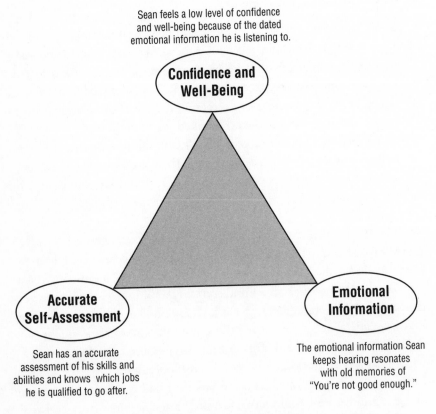

Sean feels a low level of confidence and well-being because of the dated emotional information he is listening to.

Confidence and Well-Being

Accurate Self-Assessment

Emotional Information

Sean has an accurate assessment of his skills and abilities and knows which jobs he is qualified to go after.

The emotional information Sean keeps hearing resonates with old memories of "You're not good enough."

Sean's Confidence Triangle

Viewing his situation through the Confidence Triangle enabled Sean to shift to neutral and get clear sight. He was a very practical and realistic person, who had an accurate self-assessment of his skills and abilities. However, he also had outdated messages stored in his emotional memory that produced a gut reaction of fear and negativity every time he started to think about his job search. He needed to break this old emotional habit.

The first step was to acknowledge that the old emotional information was not consistent with today's reality. Sean had confidence in his abilities to assess his credentials for the types of jobs he was interested in. He needed to stretch these strengths to also assess when his old emotional information was out of sync with today's skills. In other words, he needed to replace feelings of "Nobody will hire you" with "You are every bit as good as any other candidate and probably far more qualified than most"—realistic feelings for someone with his experience and skills.

Retraining the Body

To reprogram the retrieval of new, updated emotional information, Sean was mindful when the old messages occurred and consciously replaced them in his mind with positive messages. By staying mindful of these new messages, his body soon recognized new patterns. The old messages made his body feel tight and fearful. He told himself this feeling was not in sync with today's reality—that he should *feel* as good as his skills really are. He knew the mind reprogramming had been successfully completed when he felt a release in his body that communicated confidence. As he described the shift, I immediately heard a change in the tone of his voice to a more mellow tone. Sean recognized it, too.

As Sean made the shift to absorbing the new emotional information, he also reported a growing feeling of self-confidence and well-being. Sean now knows he needs to keep practicing this routine until it becomes an automatic reaction. He keeps a picture of the Confidence Triangle attached to his calendar so he is reminded to shift to neutral any time he feels the discomfort of old emotional information. Then he actively reprograms his feelings until he can experience a level of assurance in his body. It may take several months to build this new habit. This doesn't concern him. He knows he just needs to keep practicing. The Confidence Triangle gives him a very tangible reminder of steps to take to reinforce his new feelings of confidence.

Sean's strategy worked. The proof came when several family crises occurred that would previously have provided the alibis for Sean to stop thinking about his own career needs. Instead, he recognized that he could slow down a little to handle the crisis, yet remain ultimately committed to his job search. He deserved equal time. Ultimately, that shift in perspective led to multiple new job opportunities for Sean.

Sean's Clear Sight Plan

Sean wrote down his Clear Sight Plan to reinforce his goals and commitment, as you can see next.

Sean's Clear Sight Plan

Goal: Create new job opportunities for myself.

1. Build a network of contacts to help identify potential jobs.
2. Use the Confidence Triangle to uncover negative emotional information that may be holding me back; and reprogram myself with feelings of confidence.
3. Seek out new job possibilities that seem to fit my strength and experience.

This plan served him for about two months. Then he developed a new plan. He makes it a habit to set goals for himself every three months and identifies any potential blind spots and a Clear Sight Plan that supports his goals. He paid particular attention to the confidence associated with his emotional information.

While Sean's feelings were not in sync with his well-developed skills, Nadia had the reverse situation. She had old emotional information that

---

Why Do Highly Competent People Feel Low Confidence?

In our early years, our parents and caretakers give us signals about our feelings for ourselves. Overly demanding expectations may teach us that we can never measure up. Overprotection tells us we are incapable of accomplishing things independently. When we are encouraged to accept ourselves for who we are and to be comfortable with what we achieve according to our own expectations, we develop self-confidence. Throughout our early lives, friends and colleagues can give us the same kind of signals. Relationships that require too high expectations can lead to constant loss of confidence.

Many parents believe they are helping their children by encouraging overachievement, when they may instead be creating a life for their children of feeling emotionally inadequate.

Fortunately, we can change the voices within our heads by recognizing them as blinding influences, and focus instead on realistic challenges and good feelings about what we choose to achieve.

---

signaled strengths while her actual skills were not up to par. Nadia used the Confidence Triangle to understand why she was receiving feedback from her boss about her lack of effective team work.

Nadia Adjusts Her Sense of Reality

After graduating from college, Nadia joined her current company as a direct marketing representative. She worked hard, and her track record for attracting new business was outstanding. She was continually given raises and additional responsibility. Eventually she became responsible for all media placement for the company, had contact with others throughout the organization, and had a couple of people reporting to her. I met Nadia as her high-achieving world was about to experience some cracks.

Nadia's success had exceeded her expectations for herself. She felt confident and had a gut feeling that she was highly admired by herself and others. The emotional information she was receiving reinforced her feelings of self-confidence. She believed nothing could stop her from continually building success.

However, Nadia was not accurately reading the reactions of those around her who she worked with daily. They experienced her as a tyrant who made endless demands and never expressed appreciation for anything they did for her. No one wanted to be teamed with her on a project. She was the focus of many negative comments discussed by the water cooler.

Nadia was in the exact opposite position from Sean. He was experiencing outdated, negative emotional information about his competency that led to low confidence for someone with his strong skills. Nadia, in contrast, had dated emotional information that inflated her self-confidence. She also had an inaccurate self-assessment of her skills and abilities in the area of managing people.

Nadia's boss received so much negative feedback that he sat down and told her she was in trouble. He was tired of hearing endless complaints about how difficult she was to deal with, and wanted her to take responsibility for solving the problem. Nadia was shocked. This was the first time she had directly heard anything negative about her work. She had a blind spot the size of a crater, and had no idea how to deal with it.

Nadia followed the process of this book, and with her self-confidence still intact, ventured out to talk to her fellow workers. She told them she was trying to get feedback on her way of working with others and asked eight people to fill out the Blind Spots 360.

I used the Confidence Triangle to help Nadia shift to neutral and better understand her situation.

Nadia's Blind Spots 360 gave her more information from her colleagues than she was immediately able to process.

- She was recognized as an energetic, hardworking achiever.
- She was seen as pushing her stress on others.
- She was seen as blind to the feelings of other people and incapable of empathy.
- Her communication style was perceived as one-sided and too direct.

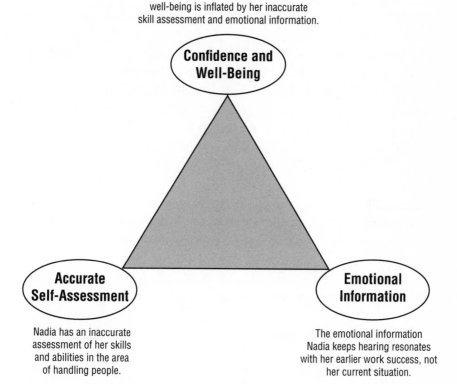

Nadia's high confidence and
well-being is inflated by her inaccurate
skill assessment and emotional information.

**Confidence and
Well-Being**

**Accurate
Self-Assessment**

**Emotional
Information**

Nadia has an inaccurate
assessment of her skills
and abilities in the area
of handling people.

The emotional information
Nadia keeps hearing resonates
with her earlier work success, not
her current situation.

Nadia's Confidence Triangle

Nadia was overwhelmed by this negative feedback. When overwhelmed, she knew she needed to shift to neutral, which she did by taking the Blind Spots Profile. The results are summarized next.

Nadia's Blind Spots Profile Model: Optimistic Image-Oriented Producer

Greatest Personal Strength: High-energy multitasker, produces many projects valued by others.

Potential Blind Spot: Constant multitasking can lead to disorganization and indecision. When pressured, can become distant, dismissive, and alienate others.

This model helped Nadia to understand why she was creating such a negative impression among her co-workers. She advanced quickly as an Optimistic Image-Oriented Producer because she used her high-energy multitasking ability for achievement. She created such a favorable impression with her boss that he promoted her; however, being so task-oriented, she distanced those around her and simply tuned them out. The only emotional information she was receiving was satisfaction about task completion. Her productivity was so high that she resonated with positive messages in her body. However, under the pressure she created for herself, she was literally ignoring everyone else, becoming distant and dismissive of them.

Nadia was stunned by this picture, particularly since she always considered herself as a feelings-oriented person. She would have to totally reprogram herself to get her co-workers on her side. She developed a goal and a Clear Sight Plan, which she called DIAL so she could keep it in her mind constantly. Each of the letters of the word DIAL represents the first word in each of her clear sight objectives. Nadia's Clear Sight Plan is outlined next.

Nadia's Clear Sight Plan

Goal: To get my co-workers to see me as supportive rather than disruptive.

1. De-stress my daily work routine to make time for attention to co-workers.
2. Initiate personal contact with people throughout the day.
3. Ask about them.
4. Listen to what they have to say.

Nadia put cards with the words Shift to Neutral on her desk, in her planner, on the screen of her computer, and in her purse. When she looked at those words, they reminded her to slow down and think about others for a moment. Throughout the day she made it a goal to stop two or three people just to ask them about their project or work. She made herself listen to their responses rather than tuning them out or going back in her mind to her own work objectives.

When we are with people and our mind is elsewhere, they immediately feel our lack of presence. It communicates "You are not as important as the things on my mind." It's often better not to be with people than to be with them and tune them out. Their emotional brains can pick up the fact that you are not really there.

Nadia estimated that her two to three contacts a day with people just to chat probably added only 20 minutes of time. This really didn't detract from the amount of work she was able to do. While she was trying to change her emotional habits, she found she had to pay a lot of attention to shifting to neutral. This took much discipline.

Over a period of three months, Nadia gradually noticed a change in her relationships with other people. At first it was as simple as recognizing their existence. Then she began to understand their priorities and simple ways to help them out while doing her own work. After a month of following her Clear Sight Plan, she went back to her boss to ask how she was doing on the negative feedback to him. He smiled and said, "I hadn't thought about it for awhile. No one's complained lately. In this case I guess no news is good news."

Choose for Yourself

How does your confidence feel about taking on your goal for success? Use the Confidence Triangle to identify an assessment of your skills and abilities and the reliability of your current emotional information. Note any changes you think need to occur. Develop an appropriate Clear Sight Plan. Note this information in your personal self-portrait.

You now know the five principles for clear sight and are ready to move to Section Four, where you'll learn strategies to turn each of the five most common blind spots into strengths.

Section Four

The Strategies for Clear Sight

You have identified your blind spots and observed how others have turned their blind spots into strengths. Now it's your turn. Each chapter of this section presents detailed strategies for one of the five most common blind spots. If you have completed the Blind Spots 360, you will have feedback from others about which of these strategies is most relevant to *your* blind spots.

It's best to pick just one chapter at a time and focus on it. Trying to read more than one chapter or develop multiple strategies can be overwhelming. Remember, focusing on two or three simple steps is the most effective way to develop Clear Sight.

Chapter 11: Clear Sight Strategy 1—Identify Strengths

Not being clear about your strengths is a major blind spot. It can undercut your confidence and reduce your energy and vitality.

- Develop your *Statement of Strengths.*

Chapter 12: Clear Sight Strategy 2—Check Old Habits

Old habit blind spots are often developed in adolescence when they prove successful in helping us reach our adolescent goals. Blind spots may keep us from realizing that these old habits are not part of who we are; they are just habits that do not serve today's goals.

- Review the *Old Habits Blind Spots Grid.*

Chapter 13: Clear Sight Strategy 3—Address Stress

We may be experiencing stress that we believe others can't see. They do see it and it interferes with our goals and relationships.

- Follow a three-step strategy to make stress work for rather than against you.

Chapter 14: Clear Sight Strategy 4—Tune Radar

We need to be aware of the nonverbal cues we send out, as well as recognize the nonverbal cues others are sending. When we communicate conflicting non-verbal signals, we lose influence.

- Learn three simple steps to tune your radar.

Chapter 15: Clear Sight Strategy 5—Connect

Our integrity and trustworthiness are often perceived by our ability to connect with other people effectively.

- Check the *Characteristics of Disconnection* and learn how to avoid them.

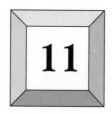

Identify Strengths

IF YOU ARE unclear about what your strengths are, you have a blind spot that can undercut the confidence you feel. You may waffle about decisions or exhibit signs of uncertainty to others. You may shrink from expressing your views or take the criticism of others too personally. This blind spot is not a case of overusing your strength, but of not recognizing the strength you already have within you.

Until this point in the book, your overused *strengths* have been the reference point for identifying your blind spots. You probably have many strengths. Marcus Buckingham and Donald Clifton in *Now, Discover Your Strengths* have identified 34 strength themes to consider. I want you to be aware of all of your strengths in facing your goals for success. They are the anchor for your self-confidence. How you *feel* about your strengths gives you an ongoing sense of well-being as challenges come your way.

In *Blind Spots* we focus specifically on strengths related to how we think and feel in the moment. These gut strengths are particularly important for quick decision-making in our speed driven world. Knowing your gut strength may also help you find what Stephen Covey in his book *The Eighth Habit* calls "your voice." Having voice means you can tap certain innate talents within yourself. Your gut strength is fundamental to your voice.

Many people I meet and work with overlook their gut strengths. Here is what I tell them:

- Gut reactions are communicated by subtle sensory feelings that require attention to understand.
- They don't get our attention because the constant noise of our minds overwhelms them.
- We can hear our gut reactions by learning to pay attention to the signals they send.
- We can test their reliability by reviewing their input against other facts.
- We can honor them by recognizing their value-added to decision making.

Your gut reactions reflect your persona, character, and personality and influence your day-to-day experience. They can be considered along with facts to give you a signal about how well what you are doing fits your understanding of who you are, what you know, and how you act. The more experience you gain, the better educated your gut strength becomes. It provides a beacon for your success, illuminating your understanding of the life choices most in sync with your principles, values, self-knowledge, and wisdom.

When you ignore your gut strengths or learn to see them as unreliable, you develop blind spots that seriously limit your potential for success.

Do You Connect with Your Strengths?

When I meet someone who is not connected to their strengths, I experience certain signs. The individual reveals a certain level of discomfort. There is a sense of hesitancy about them. They may appear businesslike, but also seem to be not quite sure of themselves. The individual may be articulate, professional, and certainly well-versed in industry and project knowledge. They work hard, but there is also a certain look in their eyes that makes me wonder if the person is comfortable in their own skin.

Monica appeared to me to be one of these people.

Anyone who met 35-year-old Monica recognized her accomplishments. She worked hard and had a resume loaded with top schools and jobs showing her climb through increasingly responsible positions in the packaged goods industry. Now a middle manager with a staff of 40, she asked me to work with her in response to some questions her boss had raised about her leadership style. She wanted me to conduct interviews with those who reported to her about their perceptions of how she was viewed as a leader. I met with each of her 10 direct reports and summarized what I learned.

Monica was viewed as hardworking and knowledgeable. She hired good people who were strong and capable. She was viewed as having high standards and doing innovative, strategic projects. But she was also perceived as defensive, skeptical, and testy at times. She would doubt those who reported to her and sometimes appeared paranoid. People saw her as a manager who was sometimes too harsh and bullying and at other times too trusting and candid with her staff. She might agree to something, but would then change her mind and not let others know of her shift.

Monica appeared hesitant to reach out to those she didn't know throughout the organization. At times she seemed power hungry and was very status conscious, dropping names of important connections. She would seem aloof and distant and then suddenly share some personal details with someone that became the gossip of the week on the floor. Those I spoke with were getting confusing cues from Monica.

My sense was that Monica's changing behaviors were rooted in an unlearned sense of self. She was not able to recognize her inner voice coming from her gut strengths. Without the depth of judgment that comes from *consciously* incorporating emotional inner information with moment-to-moment facts, Monica lacked confidence in her own decisions, vacillated in her opinions, and felt ungrounded in her own beliefs.

Monica's greatest strength according to the Blind Spots Profile, as a

Practical, Questioning Loyalty Builder, was her intellect. She would use it to test the trustworthiness of people by questioning what they were doing until she was convinced about their ability to deliver. Monica knew she tended to use her intellect, but she never owned it as a core gut strength. Instead, she worked from a blind spot. She had high standards and extensive knowledge but was constantly skeptical and second-guessing her decisions. She had to admit that even *she* was more aware of her shortcomings than her strengths. In fact, she was not able to clearly describe her strengths without a lot of hesitation.

Together we developed a statement of Monica's fundamental strengths, paying attention to understanding her gut strength as well as related strengths.

Monica's Statement of Strengths

- My mind is always testing the trustworthiness of others and scrutinizing my own judgments, which I use constructively to make wise choices. It is my gut strength.
- I am responsible, serious, and hardworking and have strong standards about what I expect from others.
- I make a commitment to support those with whom I associate.
- Whatever life brings me, I have a strong inner fortitude.
- I will to forge forward and make decisions that are in the best interests of myself and those I choose to work with.
- My choices may not always be the most popular ones, but they are well-tested and provide a solid foundation to meet any challenge head on.

This series of statements took Monica some time to think through. When it was done, she felt a burden lift. She knew that she was still prone to excessively analyzing and rethinking things all the time, but she also knew that these behaviors could be managed to make wise judgments.

The Confidence Triangle that I presented in Chapter 10 provides perspective on the shift within Monica. Prior to clearly articulating her strengths, Monica had felt a lack of confidence in herself because she didn't acknowledge her own strengths. When she had completed her statement of strengths, she began to own them. Her self-assessment became more accurate.

As she clearly articulated her strengths, she felt a sense of ease and comfort in her body. Her emotional information was reinforcing the belief in her self-assessment. In essence, the words resonated with actions she knew she would clearly take. She now held the words in her body. The Confidence Triangle below describes the shift that resulted from Monica's owning the power of her gut strength, after completing her strength statement.

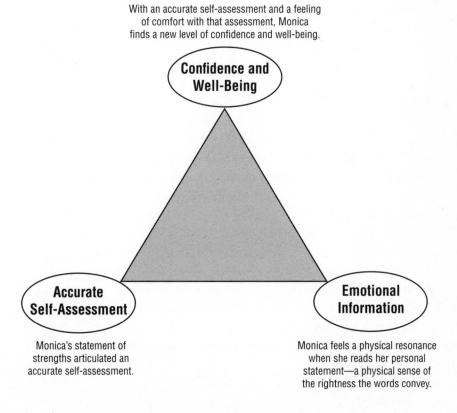

With an accurate self-assessment and a feeling of comfort with that assessment, Monica finds a new level of confidence and well-being.

Confidence and Well-Being

Accurate Self-Assessment

Monica's statement of strengths articulated an accurate self-assessment.

Emotional Information

Monica feels a physical resonance when she reads her personal statement—a physical sense of the rightness the words convey.

Monica's Confidence Triangle

In short, Monica's confidence increased not just from writing her statement, but because the words reflected what both her rational and her emotional brain communicate through a sense of rightness in her subtle body cues. The words provided her not only with a sense of purpose, but with *a feeling of the willingness to commit to action* to support those words.

Others Can Sense Your Confidence

Like Monica, you can gain confidence from recognizing your strengths. When your self-assessment of strengths is in sync with your feelings about those strengths, you will feel a connection within yourself. Others will sense it in your presence.

In their book *Leadership Presence*, ex-actors Belle Linda Halpern and Kathy Lubar describe how leaders can make an authentic connection with their colleagues, managers, and clients. These authors bring dramatic techniques to creating the natural presence of a leader. Great leaders such as George Washington, Mahatma Gandhi, Winston Churchill, and Martin Luther King Jr., each of whom had gut strength and a strong set of principles and beliefs about their cause, possessed this ability to persuade people to courses of action to which all felt a part.

While we may not all become powerful leaders, each of us has the potential of connecting to our strengths and in turn creating a presence that strengthens our relationships to other people. Whether we possess the introspective strength of a Gandhi or the expressive strength of a Martin Luther King Jr., we can draw from our strengths in a way that communicates confidence to those we work with. It is this connection of our strengths with our *feelings* about these strengths that gives us personal power.

By gaining clarity about your gut strengths, you will take the first step in understanding the hidden potential you can develop as a leader. Lack of connection to your gut strengths can lead you to communicate an uncertain, testy, skeptical impression. Belief in your gut strength will resonate in your body and communicate the essence of who you are to others.

Can Gut Strengths Be Learned in School?

How do we move from gut strength to personal power? It starts with a clear knowledge of our inner strengths. Hopefully, we learn this in our early home and school life; how these strengths are recognized or ignored will affect how we relate to ourselves from then on, as the sidebar explains.

For several years I directed a human growth and development program for adolescents. There I learned how 13-year olds can be taught to recognize their own and others' gut strengths. Students worked with a tool similar to the Blind Spots Profile to identify their gut strengths. We called these strengths their "innersense." Students interviewed parents

----

Where Do Blind Spots Come From?

When children develop a pattern of thinking, feeling, or behaving that shifts responsibility for their performance to someone or some reason outside their control, they build up blind spots that keep them from seeing the potential of their own strengths. Consider Rick, who explains to his parents when his grades drop, "The teacher doesn't like me. She always singles me out in class when I don't understand something. I don't want to go to class."

Shifting Rick's perspective away from the teacher's not liking him back to his taking responsibility for his performance, supports Rick to problem solve. A helpful parental suggestion might be, "Let's talk to your teacher together to work out a plan for improving your understanding of math." This approach moves Rick back to problem solving in math and halts the development of blind spots.

In reality the teacher may really not like Rick and may allow this to influence his or her teaching. However, if Rick accepts this as a reason to allow himself to fail, he can develop a blind spot that unconsciously reinforces his vulnerabilities rather than his strengths. He may develop a habit of seeing barriers instead of solutions and retreat into himself rather than proactively attacking the problem.

----

and classmates to gather details about how these personal strengths added value to their family and friendships, and wrote papers about their conclusions.

The appreciation of shared strengths created a joyful and productive middle-school classroom environment. As students better understood the Blind Spots Profile model they chose, they became the expert on presenting it to the class. Most students loved the opportunity to share their stories and get enthusiastic support from classmates for characteristics they saw in themselves.

Some of the students found school naturally brought out the best in them. (Refer to Chapter 4 for a description of strengths and blind spots.) Those who identified with the Optimistic Image-Oriented Producer strengths believed the more they accomplished, the more they would be valued. They thrived in a school environment where club leadership roles and school projects were numerous. The Responsible High-Standards Builders motivated to reach high standards also loved the school environment where they could find the right way to do things.

The more introspective students struggled sometimes, feeling misunderstood by their peers, and often isolated. They gained confidence as they shared their thinking with other students. For example, one female with Reserved Analytical Strategist gut strengths was relieved to explain to her classmates that her preference to remain detached from others in moments of tension and crisis didn't mean she didn't have feelings for them. She just performed at her best when she saw the details and big picture of what was happening. She told me later that until that moment she had always thought something was wrong with her.

One Empathic Conflict-Avoiding Diplomat whose life revolved around horseback riding was true to her natural ability to resolve conflicts and walk in other people's shoes. Her mother was concerned that she was avoiding the social scene in favor of her horse. One step ahead of her mother, this young woman explained that while she really preferred time with her horse to the catty chatting of her peers, she knew her parents needed to know that she was popular and had friends. Her solution was limiting her riding to two days a week, and staying at school other afternoons with the girls so "my parents won't worry."

Both male and female Warm Relationship Builders were at the center of the social scene, although they felt devalued by an academic environment that seemed only to value good grades and not human connection.

Two other models of students appeared to have a more difficult time adapting to school. The Assertive Get-It-Doner adolescents had an instinctive sense of how power was exercised in the classroom. If they were not feeling confident and valued, they often chose a path of rebellion against the teacher. When a teacher chose to push back in a power game, these kids could be relentless in distracting other students and defying the teachers. In my classroom, I was careful to explain to these students how their natural charismatic leadership skills could be helpful in class discussions. When these students felt valued, they were very effective in leading meaningful but disciplined discussions among their peers.

The other students who sometimes had a difficult time adjusting to school were those who saw themselves as Energetic New Direction Risk Takers, who valued excitement and adventure. They simply found school boring much of the time and became distracted.

As young students or adults, how we grow to *feel about our strengths* is clearly conditioned by our environment. It's a lot easier to feel appreciated when our personalities and natural strengths are valued within our environment. However, today environments are complex enough and shift enough that we need to prepare ourselves for any environment. That preparation comes from living comfortably with the environment within ourselves.

Do You Know What Your Gut Strengths Are?

Whether you were one of those students who loved and were loved by their teachers, or one of those rebels or adventurers who could have skipped the school years, you need to be clear on where your strengths lie today.

While many people don't see or may resist facing their blind spots, many are also unable to describe their inner personal strengths. They can prepare a resume. They can work hard and be competitive. But they may not recognize what strengths remain when all the trappings of prestige, money, and accomplishment are taken away.

Want to better define your inner strengths? Here's an exercise that brings time-tested results.

Assignment: Create Your Statement of Strengths

Describe your greatest strengths that underlie everything you do in every situation you find yourself.

Make note of it as part of your personal self-portrait.

Observe the strengths that you and other people see in you. Then do the following:

- Write a paragraph about yourself describing your strengths. If you find it difficult to start, write it in the third person as if you are describing a stranger. Read the description you've written out loud, and see how it resonates. Do you have a gut sense that the description is authentic?
- If the description doesn't feel good to you, readjust it until you feel a sense of confidence when you read it. Don't allow the words to overpower or underpower the sense of who you are.

Your statement can be designed in any format. Some people like lists, others prose. You can use Monica's Statement of Strengths as a model. It's the resonance that counts, not the form. One of my clients kept his statement of strengths, which was written in his favorite style of bullet points, next to his day planner. He had been working for several months to gain the confidence that his experience and training suggested he should feel. Unfortunately he learned at a young age that *what he produced* was more important than *who he was*. To reach the success that his personal potential suggested, he knew he needed to feel and express his personal power. Every time he read his strengths statement, he felt the sense of knowing that he was connected to the source of that power.

So how will your strengths sustain you in the worst of times? Chapter 12 will help you to see old habits that may be getting in your way.

12

Check Old Habits

SOMETIMES WE HAVE blind spots that were formed so early in life that they feel like a part of who we are. These habits have shaped our way of being and our identity. Yet our life has moved on and what was successful behavior for a 13-year-old may be totally inappropriate for a 35-year old.

Remember Joey from the first chapter? He had gotten a lot of attention in high school for his entertaining way of being with other people. However, his gift of gab and needing to be the center of attention was not as attractive for a 30-year-old trying to work efficiently with a team. The team found Joey high maintenance in spite of his gangbuster sales results.

Old habits blind spots are often the most difficult to recognize because they feel so comfortable and familiar:

- These blind spots feel like strengths now because in earlier situations, they probably were.
- Giving up an old habit is like giving up an old friend, whom we may have outgrown but still feel connected to.
- By identifying these habits and changing their influence, we gain tremendous new energy.

While there are many different types of old patterns, I provide a quick overview with a model of four that I have encountered frequently in my clients.

Four Old Habits Blind Spots

To understand these old habits, think back to a high school setting, and imagine how it felt to deal with other adolescents your age. You may have been shy and retiring and got along by being a person of few words. Or perhaps you were emotionally expressive and became the center of everything. Or you may have been one of those conscientious, responsible students who completed every assignment with perfection. Or you

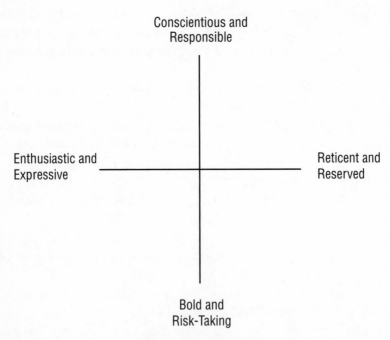

Old Habits Blind Spots Grid:
Do You Overdo Your Behavior in Any of the Four Grid Directions?

were the bold, creative risk taker who came up with ingenious ideas, but pushed the rules and delivered the unexpected.

Most likely you were some combination of these and have probably adapted adolescence behaviors to adult life. But every so often, there may be some habit that worked then, but doesn't work now. That's where your blind spot may reside.

The Old Habits Blind Spots Grid identifies four patterns of behavior that when overused create blind spots. It helps to boil these patterns down to a simple perspective.

All four of these patterns can be very positive. When overused, they can become blinding, even wreaking havoc on your credibility. Look closely at each of these four patterns. Probably only one or two will apply to you.

Conscientious and Responsible

If you think you are extremely conscientious and responsible, read the description of Martin next and see if he sounds anything like you. If you don't consider yourself particularly conscientious and responsible, move on to the next section.

As the oldest child of five children, Martin, 33, grew up feeling responsible. He was a role model for the family. A straight A student in school, he was head of a number of organizations and was always available to support community projects. He did the same in college and got a job upon graduation with a high-tech company where his career continued to grow. He was the picture of responsibility and fulfillment of duty. He was rated very highly by every boss he worked for as he progressed in the high-tech field.

I met Martin when he was facing his first sense of failure.

If you have the same sense of standards and responsibility as Martin, you may wonder where the blind spots may be hiding that could block his success. They didn't show up until Martin began to manage increasing numbers of people.

Martin genuinely tried to be a great manager. He would meet with his team regularly, encouraged them to develop their skills, and attempted to give balanced feedback about their work. However, the demands of deadlines and results always pulled him to do things his way—the right way. People who reported to Martin felt constrained and became discouraged by not having the freedom to initiate their own ideas.

When the stress was greatest, Martin would become so precise in his directions that others felt smothered and discouraged. His group's results began to reflect their work style—tired and predictable. In his role as head of new technology development, Martin was expected to produce innovative solutions. His disconnection to himself and those in his organization was leading to a lack of energy needed for producing new ideas!

How Can You Become Less Responsible?

If you share Martin's need to do things the right way in the extreme, you will probably experience your blind spots when you feel a sense of failure for the first time in your life. Since you've always been able to use your high standards to meet and exceed others' expectations, you may feel totally overwhelmed when this strategy starts to work against you. The insight you need to build clear sight is to share responsibility. This may be very hard for you to do at first.

The overly responsible dance goes like this. While you may tell someone you want to develop shared goals, secretly you will find flaws in what the other person offers. (Of course, no one has as high standards as you do!) This will lead to your sending nonverbal cues that communicate the other person's inferiority and lack of expertise for the task. The individual will respond by withdrawing from you or passing the job back for you to do in a way that meets your standards. Then you will feel abandoned and have a justified need to become more responsible. See how this pattern can repeat itself?

Here's a sample clear sight plan that might get you started on a path to greater balance.

Your Clear Sight Plan

Your Goal: Share responsibility with others.

1. Hold discussions with people about how you can share responsibilities for assignments, being clear on expected results in advance.
2. Hold your feedback when someone brings something back to you that doesn't meet your personal expectations. (Ask yourself if the work is just good enough to be acceptable.)
3. Thank the individual for the contribution they have made to the task.
4. Get planned exercise to take out your feelings about frustrated standards in a positive way.

Ultimately, you will find that by following this approach you will be expressing value for inclusion of others. They will see you as someone whom they want to work with. You will experience a new meaning for "responsibility"—one that refers not only to standards but also to energy and synergy.

In describing the strength of a basketball coach, author Tom Market identified coach Phil Jackson as an example of an inclusive manager, one who motivates others. People excluded from decision-making feel unimportant and are thus less motivated. This is what happens when you assume total responsibility for calling all the plays for others. By changing your intention to give others more responsibility, you increase motivation and stimulate more exciting results.

The greatest difficulty you face as an overly responsible individual is the inner task of feeling that it is acceptable to lower your own standards. That inner critic of yours may begin to harp on you to feel guilty. You may feel inadequate. Stick with it. Remember you are changing what has *felt* normal to you all your life. Over several months or even a year, your feelings about responsibility will begin to shift.

The opposite style from the overly conscientious and responsible individual is the one who is wildly bold and risk taking. Others might even describe this person as irresponsible.

Bold and Risk Taking

If you think you are one of the people who are bold and risk taking, read the description of Ashley and see if she sounds like you.

Ashley, 35, was the middle child of three. She was the one in school whom everyone envied, as she left her assignments till the night before they were due and crammed for brilliant results. She was a strong athlete and was able to get that uncanny shot in the last moment of the basketball quarter that won the game. In many ways, she appeared bigger than life. Everyone was both afraid and in awe of her.

She just had a gift for making the bold move that no one expected. For example, even though her grades were just solid and SATs were okay, she managed to get into an Ivy League school. She said it was because of her interview. She made a strong and lasting first impression.

I met her at a business school alumnae function where I was participating in a panel discussion on career development.

If you are a bold risk taker like Ashley, you may not realize how alone you really are until you have your first failure. Let's explore the dynamics of how this unfolded for Ashley.

Upon graduation from college, Ashley got a job for an investment management company where she distinguished herself by coming up with unique investment strategies, which made Ashley and the firm a great deal of money.

People in the firm found Ashley a bit too quick-witted for their comfort zone. Her strategies were a little too innovative. Her self-confident manner, which communicated that she wasn't afraid of anything, made her peers a little suspect. While others welcomed Ashley's contributions to the bottom line, they found her thinking tested the limits of the firm.

No one wanted to kill the golden egg producer so as long as she continued producing; everyone stood back and applauded her performance. However, one day her strategy failed and the company lost a bundle on her ill-advised plan. Then her peers stood back, gloated with one another, and let her flop. Her peers and bosses, who had long found her style of operating too risky and opinionated for their tastes, did nothing to help her. They let her hang out to dry.

Truthfully, Ashley had isolated herself by not building bridges with others in the firm; however she still was shocked by the pleasure others seemed to find in her defeat.

Reaching the Tipping Point

Secrets to Winning at Office Politics by Marie McIntyre describes the predicament of becoming The Problem as Ashley did. Her risk taking and lone ranger behaviors started consuming a disproportionate share of her managers' attention. Managers had been expecting fallout from Ashley's style for so long that a tipping point of concern had formed. They knew it was only a matter of time before a failure would occur. They simply waited for the evidence to support their position.

If you are a high-achieving risk takers, realize that your ways may create friction with others who are not as bold and adventurous. They may be suspicious of your attitude and way of thinking on a large scale. Expect in advance that they may not be supportive when you fail.

Understand that extreme risk taking ways can isolate you even in an environment that prides itself on risk taking. To prevent the kind of isolation and alienation that Ashley experienced, start building up the relationships that will be there to help you through tough times. Next is a clear sight plan that can help.

Your Clear Sight Plan

Your Goal: Strengthen your relationships.

1. Meet regularly with key people just to get on their wavelength.
2. Reach out to others to develop joint strategies so you're not always going it alone.
3. Recognize the contributions of others and don't present yourself as a lone ranger.

Following this plan, you will be able to build the relationships that will make others comfortable with you and your work style. Don't make radical, sudden changes but slowly reach out to others. Share your thinking to avoid appearing like a peacock in the midst of a lot of other people who have egos as well.

Both Ashley and Martin had arrived at a tipping point in the attitudes of how others perceived them. Consider for a moment where you are in reaching a tipping point of opinion in the minds of others you work with as you read the following story.

Are You At Your Tipping Point?

Your success in any organization is seldom determined overnight. While your ability to produce results gets you into the game, your future success is largely determined by people's comfort level in relying on you. Whether you are a boss, peer, client, or member of a work group, your ability to be seen as someone who is a catalyst for constructive solutions makes a difference.

Your reputation builds slowly and then reaches its tipping point as the many people you come into contact with develop a similar reading of who you are. This is the tipping point, when you are generally seen as valued, a problem, or something nondescript in the middle.

Signs of being valued are clear. People seek out your opinion, share information with you, and listen carefully to what you say. You're asked to serve on special assignments or sit in on confidential conversations. You feel engaged. Signs of problem status are also clear. You operate alone a lot. You are excluded from meetings, not asked for your opinion, and are left out of the loop of conversations about what is going on.

If you are not currently a part of either of these scenarios, you are probably in transition. People are observing and experiencing what it is like to work with you. This is the time to access your blind spots, and understand how they fit into the culture of this organization and values of its people. Assess your possibilities for success before the organization forms its opinion of you. Make sure you are on the road to being valued.

People others don't like to work with ultimately end up as losers in the workplace, particularly as resources diminish and stress increases. Regardless of your brilliance or track record, if you are difficult sooner or later those in the organization will find a way to live without you. That was certainly a problem Ashley faced. It is the reason why operating from old blind spots can become such a liability for even high-achieving producers.

The next pair of blind spots relates to emotional expression. On one extreme we have those who are overly expressive and on the other end those who don't seem to emote at all.

Emotionally Expressive

If you think you are one of the people who are highly emotionally expressive, read about the problems Dylan faced in his job. If you are more reticent in style, move on to the next section.

Dylan was always full of enthusiasm. From childhood, he had always been the one who grabbed the attention of the crowd. He was the main character in all the school plays and was in the popular crowd in high school. He motivated the lacrosse and football teams with his rallying cries. Passionate, charming, and entertaining, Dylan immediately engaged anyone he met in conversation. He had many friends and was invited to everyone's party. He attended a small liberal arts college where he became president of his fraternity. While he didn't distinguish himself in the classroom, he was a solid student and graduated with a major in history.

I was introduced to Dylan by his manager at the company where he held a sales management role.

At 30, Dylan was a sales manager for an international luxury jewelry retailer. He was recognized early for his ability to connect with customers, to understand their interests and needs and to close big ticket item sales. Watching him interact with customers was like a stage performance. This is what helped to build and maintain his success.

As a salesperson, Dylan's blind spots were rarely seen. As a manager and peer who had daily contact with others, Dylan began to be perceived as more volatile. He would attempt to motivate others to meet sales goals. When they fell short, he exploded and became angry. The usually charming and engaging man would become enraged and almost abusive to people.

There were several incidents of employees being driven to tears by one of his tirades. He would leave the room and feel totally revitalized while those he had been with were devastated. Dylan would have little memory of the incident, while the subject of his momentary wrath would feel traumatized for weeks.

Dylan would also present a hot and cold attitude toward members of the team. When someone was new, Dylan would wine and dine them and include them in all kinds of personal conversations. He would promote their objectives and enthusiastically listen to their ideas. As time passed, someone new would attract his attention and his involvement would shift. These mood shifts left others feeling betrayed and discarded.

Finding Balance

If you are like Dylan, you probably are not aware of how your volatile, up-and-down behavior is viewed by others as untrustworthy and undependable. To avoid building this type of negative reputation for yourself, develop a clear sight plan similar to the one following.

Your Clear Sight Plan

Your Goal: Build a more even tempered, consistent level of expressiveness with people in day-to-day communications.

1. Meet regularly with all people without showing favor to one over another.
2. Develop strategies for channeling expressive behavior such as regular exercise.
3. Build time into your schedule between meetings with people to shift to neutral and feel a sense of balance within yourself.

While your expressive behavior can be energizing to others, you need to develop a range of ways to approach people with consistency. Getting an administrative system in place to help you keep track of work, not personalities, is important. Anger management techniques may also help you. Most importantly, watch your stress levels, for they can lead you to overly expressive behavior that creates long-lasting impressions that can ruin your reputation. Don't allow your expressiveness to create a tipping point of opinion that works against you.

The final old habit relates to behavior that is reserved and unexpressive in the extreme.

Reticent and Reserved

If you see yourself as reticent and reserved much of the time, consider the problems that Hailey faced.

> Hailey was a quiet, thoughtful young woman. She had often enjoyed playing alone as a child. In school, she was a good student, had a few close friends, and seemed to be interested in subjects like English and history where there were complex situations to understand. She decided in high school that she would like to be a psychologist.
>
> She attended a large university where she majored in liberal arts and was a member of the choir and modern dance clubs. At 28 Hailey was working as a researcher for a large package goods company. She liked the research field, and found that hypothesis development and testing suited her interests. But she was increasingly uncomfortable as a project leader of her group, where she was getting negative feedback about her disinterest in others' contributions. She asked me to help her understand what was going on.

Some people found Hailey unapproachable and cold, didn't think she supported their efforts publicly, and frankly never knew where she stood. She seemed so quiet and standoffish. She, on the other hand, figured everyone knew what their job was. She didn't see any need to congratulate people for what they were expected to do as part of their regular responsibilities.

The difficulty with being quiet like Hailey is that people don't know where you stand, and therefore may learn to distrust you. Reputations are built on trust. Following is a Clear Sight Plan that can help you to avoid Hailey's dilemma.

Your Clear Sight Plan

Your Goal: Increase visibility, informal communication, and presentation skills.

1. Increase the information you relate to others about their contributions.
2. Take a public speaking course to develop expressive capabilities.
3. Meet more regularly on an informal basis with others so they get to know you better and don't see you as so aloof.

This plan will help you to become visible. While you may feel more in control when you keep your feelings to yourself, others may read your behavior as cold and lacking interest in them. When you say nothing, others can imagine that something is wrong. By sharing your views a bit more with others, they will become more comfortable with you. You will build people's trust and confidence in you.

Recognizing Your Own Old Habits

You probably identified with one or at most two of these four old habits. If you identified with more than two, you are communicating mixed signals to other people. You probably have a bind spot that has blocked you from developing a clear sense of who you are. You need to stop and shift to neutral to examine how others are seeing you.

If you are like most other people, you find one or two of the Old

Habits Blind Spots apply to you. You can identify them further by using the methods of this book. Think about these questions:

- What did you do in high school or college that got the attention of your teachers and friends? How would they describe you then?
- Is this description something that would work in your favor in your work world today?
- If a gap exists between these two questions, think about how you can resolve it.

Make a note of your answers in your personal self-portrait.

After considering any old habits you need to bring into balance, you're ready to face the stresses of today's world by reading Chapter 13.

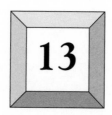

13

Address Stress

STRESS IS OFTEN the catalyst for overusing our strengths and moving us into our blind spots zones. How we respond to stress may blind us to the conflicting messages we send to others.

Whether we experience stress as pressure, tension, strain, anxiety, worry, or trauma, these feelings can lead us to unconscious behavior patterns that keep us from reaching our goals. Sometimes stress leads to simply wearing ourselves down and burning out. We don't realize we're in the downward spiral until it's too late to pull ourselves out easily. At other times, we believe we have stress in check; however others see us differently. To them our erratic, distracted, withdrawn, or exhausted behavior undercuts our credibility.

- Constant unchecked stress can make us inflexible, overusing our strengths, increasing our blind spots, and undercutting our relationships every day.
- By becoming aware of how we communicate stress and learning how to channel it constructively, we move out of our blind spots and back into conscious choices.
- When we manage stress in a way that enhances our relationships, we are able to help others we work with to manage their stress.

- When stress is ignored, it can undercut the central purpose of our lives.

Every organization is affected by stress levels today. It is a major factor influencing the energy and productivity of both individuals and the workplace as a whole. More than 90,000 people have responded to the Full Engagement Inventory, a survey that assesses how well they are managing life energy for performance and productivity. Sixty-five percent of these respondents reveal a personal energy crisis that interferes

---

North Pole News *Exclusive*

Does Santa Have a Blind Spot?

What's happening to Santa these days? One of his closest friends observed, "We always could rely on Santa's cheerful disposition and constant attention to meeting the needs of each little boy and girl. But recently he seems distant and almost robotic—putting children on his knee to hear their wish list but appearing not to really listen. The children often walk away stunned and a little confused."

Santa's situation is common to many leaders today. Most are aware of their increased personal stress. However, most also underestimate the toll that their stress is placing on those around them. This blind spot, if ignored over time, can seriously affect morale and motivation. Santa probably still believes he is being seen as a jolly old elf; however, others may be seeing their cherished Santa more like the unpopular Grinch.

How can Santa regain his jolly old self? The first step is to recognize that stress-related blind spots are common to many high-achieving people. He needs to take time to consider how his blind spots are operating. He may need to make some fundamental changes in how he manages his work. Most importantly, he needs to spend a little time each day making sure he is best using his energy to support the vision and purpose of his life. Christmas cheer depends on it.

As the Claus family heads for the North Pole Spa on December 26, it is our hope that he takes the time to get fresh perspective on his mission. You can be sure the North Pole News will monitor this situation closely—gathering our interviews and checking them twice!

---

with work and home life. What distinguishes the 6 percent who report the self-confidence and vision that comes from managing their energy most effectively is *their ability to set aside time every day to link their activities to personal or professional mission.*

Your mission statement, which we discuss in detail in Chapter 18, is simply a couple of sentences describing the one or two central objectives or purposes that are the goals of your life at this time. It provides a way to constantly remind ourselves of the central reasons we are expending our energy. It gives us perspective and a clear sense of priority. Every individual needs to note this lesson. Even Santa Claus, as the story on the previous page explains, is touched by the relationship of stress to his long-term mission!

When even Santa Claus's relationships are affected by the constant pressure and stress of our lives, how can the rest of us learn to handle it?

How Do You Express Stress?

While you may feel that your stress is being expressed only within yourself, that is seldom the case. If you are feeling continually stressed, you are communicating it to others in any number of ways.

One common stress reaction is to become supercautious, conservative, and careful in your choices. To avoid being criticized, you avoid making decisions or follow procedures to the letter of the law. You may appear tolerant of others' mistakes until one day you flare up from all the bottled stress you have been holding. Co-workers may find this sudden behavior change shocking. They may feel confused because they never know when you will become hypercritical. To avoid your criticism, they will tiptoe around you or avoid contact.

Another common stress reaction is to become angry with others. You may blame them for your own mistakes. You may forget things you said. If you are one of these people, you probably realize that you were angry, but you probably significantly underestimate the effects you are having on others. You may think you expressed a concern to someone, while the person you yelled at feels you "went ballistic." Others may even begin to describe you as abusive.

A third common stress behavior is wavering between two reactions, such as first getting enthusiastic about a project or person and then suddenly becoming disappointed. When you give mixed or changing signals like this, people may try to avoid you or may not follow through on projects you work on together. This multiplies the stress on everyone you come into contact with.

Each of these stress reactions is associated with a blind spot that prevents you from being aware of your actions. Whichever pattern represents your way of unconsciously expressing stress, you can develop clear sight to modify it.

A Circle of Stress

Stress creates more stress when it is not managed effectively. When you unconsciously express stress to other people, they start their second-guessing ways to avoid your stress reaction. This slows down productivity and often results in your feeling even more stress as your efficiency decreases. As your work piles up, you find that you're working harder and longer hours. You don't have time to engage in stress-reducing activities like going to the gym or seeing friends. You slowly become tired, miserable, and feel that you have no way out of this box you have created for yourself. People who work with you also feel very frustrated and their morale can suffer.

Reviewing the results of your Blind Spots 360 will help you to get more information about how people view your stress handling. Look to see if others recognize these stress-related behaviors in your relationships.

- Getting hypercritical and annoyed by little things.
- Becoming overly cautious and fretful.
- Having mood swings—excited one moment, disengaged the next.
- Becoming difficult to please.
- Pushing stress on others.

This information lets you see how your stress behaviors are seen by others. However you are expressing stress, there are three things you can do in your Clear Sight Plan to more effectively manage it.

Your Clear Sight Plan

1. Identify Strengths: Increase confidence by focusing on your real strengths rather than shortcomings.
2. Increase Time to Relax: Find a different way to better organize what you do.
3. Balance Energy: Reexamine how and when you use, deplete, and refuel your energy.

Step 1: Identify Strengths

Recognizing your strengths will not only help to raise your self-confidence, it can be a step toward stress reduction. What is your statement of strengths? If you haven't yet written one down, imagine one for yourself right now. Here's an example of part of the statement of strengths that Monica developed in Chapter 11.

> My mind is always testing the trustworthiness of others and scrutinizing my own judgments, which I use constructively to make wise choices. It is my gut strength.

When Monica viewed this statement, she was able to let go of her anxiety and shift to neutral: putting herself mentally in a neutral place where she could be nonjudgmental about herself and others. Once in neutral she could stop and consider her activities of the moment. If she was wavering on her own judgment, she reminded herself to rely on her own sense of inner authority. She said, "Monica, trust your self; your gut sense of this situation is good enough. Don't second-guess your gut strength."

You, like Monica, need to feel confidence in your own strengths. Learn to distinguish between two different inner voices. One is the voice of anxiety, fear, and uncertainty. This leads to blind spots that make you second-guess yourself and others. This can lead you to feeling hassled and diminished. In this state you may unnecessarily question yourself, placing yourself in a stress zone.

The other voice comes from your gut strength. Listen to this voice to sense the rightness or wrongness in what you are doing. After all, the cumulative emotional information that fuels your inner strength comes from experience. Check your gut feeling against the facts and decide quickly about your course of action. And remember a couple of sure stress producers: Perfection is too high a standard for day in and day out. Avoid redoing work. Don't procrastinate or delay decisions. Go with your gut, unless you sense something that *strongly* suggests another course of action.

Be true to your strength. It takes practice. Read your strength statement often. Leave it in an obvious place such as by a desk clock or calendar that you often check. Realize that sometimes your gut reaction may not indicate the best choice. That's okay. Some decisions may not be perfect, but over time you get far more benefit from quick decision making than from flip-flopping and doubt. People who work with you will recognize the consistency of your actions and realize that it's okay for you not to be perfect.

Now you're ready for Step 2 of your clear sight plan.

Step 2: Increase Relaxation

Only when your mind is truly empty can it really relax. A full mind may be part of your stress-related problems. Your job may include hundreds of projects and commitments that you feel you need to be on top of and follow up on. Many of these mental commitments operate on a partly conscious level, but your mind is processing them nonetheless. It's like the RAM on your computer. You may be word-processing a document, but in the background your computer is also searching for viruses, communicating with your e-mail provider, and completing security procedures. Similarly your brain keeps track of anything that you haven't finished, from your laundry in the washer, to the tickets you have for the opera, to the open projects that require next steps.

Remember that every thought is accompanied by a feeling that the mind compresses into a sense of cumulative experience that gives us a gut reaction. It's easy to see how we can feel a sense of overload from the hundreds of open items that are in our mental RAM.

David Allen, consultant and author of *Getting Things Done*, believes that productivity is directly proportional to our ability for relaxation. Relaxation comes when the mind is clear and thoughts are organized.

Transfer Open Items from Your Mind to Your Management System

When we hold a task in our minds, the mind keeps it in mental RAM. Real productivity can only result from having a way to capture unfinished items outside your mind, so that you can come back and regularly sort through them. By implementing such a trusted management system, which takes some effort, you can free up your mind to deal with things you need to focus on that are most important to the outcomes you wish to reach.

Time management and calendar management were once methods of choice for control and relaxation. They no longer are sufficient to deal with the amount of commitments that come our way through e-mail, voice mail, and in-baskets, which set in motion new commitments from hour to hour that can rearrange the initial plan for the day. You need *an all-inclusive management system* that allows you to keep constant track of all these commitments.

Our mind cannot relax until all of these commitments are captured in our management system in a way we are sure *we can revisit them*. This must include an orchestrated integration of all our organizing approaches: e-mail, voice mail, in-basket, computer, and vanilla folder filing systems. Every request coming into us must be captured in a way that we can get it off our mind by knowing we have a way to get back to it at an appropriate future time.

Allen sees *outcome thinking* as essential. Rather than thinking sequentially in terms of next steps for things on a checklist, we must think in terms of the outcome we want and what is the next important step to reach that outcome. We then set priorities by the outcomes that are most important to us.

If you're still working in a mode of looking at each individual project you work on separately and sequentially, you may need to rethink your perspective. To reduce stress, you need to be able to look *both within each project and across all projects simultaneously* to determine what requires your immediate attention. Once this decision is made for the moment, record it in some way such as a computer log incorporated into your overall management system approach. Only when something is recorded can you put it out of your mind and relax.

During the day regularly review which outcomes are most important and adjust your activities. At each decision point, record desired outcomes in your management system. Whatever your management system approach, you will slowly learn to transfer commitments from your mind to the system, so that you can *feel* relaxation and control in the moment.

Stop thinking about whole projects and focus on the most important outcomes of the next two hours, the next month, or your entire life, whichever outcome is most important to you in this moment. Transfer all of these commitments from your mind to your management system, which you can review regularly to reset your outcome priorities. Things not of immediate importance stay in the management system for future reference. They don't disturb your peace of mind.

Second-guessing yourself about your daily work simply is no longer allowed. Focus on results. Remember the third principle of clear sight, Simply Focus on Success. Make decisions about the most important outcome in the moment with the help of your gut strengths and a method of work management that you feel confident about.

The shift from feeling constantly responsible to feeling that everything needs to be off your mind and into a computer log may at first make you feel out of control. Slowly you'll realize that a free mind is actually the only way to gain control and relaxation in the long run.

Rethink Standards

To find time to relax, you may have to rethink your entire philosophy of setting standards. If you were trained in the school that says "anything worth doing is worth doing well," you may need to reconsider. High standards are important, but the quantity of your work just may not allow you to have high standards for everything you do. Time management will not solve this problem. You may have to begin thinking in terms of *acceptable quality*, not perfection, and begin setting your focus and attention on that.

Remember also that every outcome in your management system requires an associated action in this moment, for example:

- Some activities can be delayed or deferred until a later date.
- Others can be delegated or moved elsewhere.
- Some activities do require your attention.
- You need to know the results of some projects but not additional information.
- Some people require your attention.

Keep your options open. While some outcomes require the high standards that you may prefer, learn how to accept "good enough" for the bulk of your workload.

Step 3: Balance Energy

The third clear sight strategy is to balance your energy to reduce stress.

In their book *The Power of Full Engagement*, Dr. Jim Loehr and Tony Schwartz have developed a theory about the effect of using the full potential of one's personal energy. They believe that the key to managing stress lies in *managing your energy not in managing your time*. Those 6 percent out of 90,000 people they studied, who were using their energy most productively, were also distinguished by their setting aside time every day to make sure their activities were linked to their personal and professional mission.

If you belong to the 65 percent of respondents in the Full Engagement Inventory who are described as "disengaged," you probably lack sufficient physical fitness, rest, and recovery. You also probably forgo any sense of personal mission. When sleep and exercise are added back to your routine, you will report much lower stress. With a sense of mission you will use your energy fully.

As you focus on strengths and set priorities by outcomes, make use of your energy an important outcome. Program exercise time at the gym and sleep into your routine ahead of other activities. This may require a gradual transition. Take it in steps. Begin to get to the gym once a week. Over the course of two months, increase your visits to twice a week. You'll find you sleep more soundly.

Moving away from old stressful habits is a gradual change. Program changes in work outcomes through your management system. Take five minutes each day before sleep to review whether you have used your strengths effectively or are regressing into the old habit of second-guessing yourself. Keep a journal to record these reflections. Also keep track of your sleep and exercise patterns.

Tracking Results

Once a week, review your initial clear sight plan, which set these changes in motion. Keep a chart or journal tracking your own stress levels. Ask people you live and work with whether they are seeing the changes in your stress management approach. How did they experience your stress in the past? How is it affecting them now? What else can you do to change it? Be forthright about your goals and listen carefully to their reactions. You'll probably find that the more you encourage their reactions, the more they will be responsive to making changes in their own stress management approach that will benefit you.

Slowly, over time, you'll find that the level of stress you feel will decrease. If you take a few minutes each day to think about your most important priorities for yourself, you'll find that you are more constantly aware of what is important. You'll begin to think in terms of outcomes, not just activities. Instead of seeming tense or fretful all the time, you'll begin to feel calm and focused.

This will be a very significant period of personal growth in your life. You may find your confidence increasing as you go from self-doubt to being comfortable with yourself. You are learning to manage stress by keeping it out of your body and into your management system. You may experience a new level of trust with co-workers. Most of all, you will begin to see new possibilities for your work as well as your life.

Before moving on to Chapter 14 review the strategies we set in your clear sight plan for reducing stress:

- Do you know what gut strengths you can rely on for quick decision making?
- Do you have a management system in place that allows you to relax by getting all incoming needs for follow-up off your mind and onto a list?
- Are you using your energy most efficiently, by getting sufficient rest and exercise and by checking daily to see if what you are doing is in line with your personal mission?

Think about which step is most important for you to take to increase your relaxation and reduce your stress. Add this to the personal self-portrait you are developing by going through each chapter.

As you take control of your stress, you're ready in Chapter 14 to consider how and what you *resonate*.

Tune Radar

WHEN OUR RADAR is tuned, we synchronize what we say with how we say it in a way that has positive impact. When our radar is untuned, we miss the resonance or dissonance of our communication with others. This blind spot can create a negative chain reaction decreasing our potential for success. It occurs when we think we're communicating a well-thought-out message, but our nonverbal cues are contradictory.

- When others perceive conflicting nonverbal cues from us, we lose credibility.
- When we communicate conflicting nonverbal signals, regardless of the authority of our role or position, we lose influence.
- Our inconsistency can seriously undercut our trustworthiness.

Radar works on both sides of relationships. We need to be conscious of the nonverbal signals we send out but also be aware of the nonverbal signals others are communicating. Our radar interprets and communicates influence.

Influence is power in today's work world. As the business environment changes moment to moment with the speed of information, the structure of organizations is becoming more elastic. Power is exercised not only through position and role, but by the influence that comes from the strength of one's relationships and one's adaptability in changing circumstances.

To succeed in this environment we must build relationships quickly and get teams moving spontaneously. Those with the ability to quickly establish credibility and motivate others are the people primed for success. They know how to engage people to follow, always keeping their radar tuned.

The Importance of Influence

The ability to influence people to act has long been recognized as important. In 1937, when Dale Carnegie first published *How to Win Friends and Influence People,* he and his publisher expected the book to be a modest seller. Instead it was an overnight success that touched an innate public nerve. Indeed Carnegie's fundamental influence techniques are still very relevant today: (1) Don't criticize, condemn, or complain; (2) Give honest and sincere appreciation; and (3) Arouse in the person an eager want.

In the twenty-first century, the subject of influence continues to gain attention. In their book *Executive EQ,* Robert Cooper and Ayman Sawaf discuss how business leaders are moving from an emphasis on planning and prediction to shared responsibility and purpose. These new leaders embrace leadership by influence and recognize the role of *resonance* in motivating others.

Resonance suggests that emotions can be passed from one person to another in an unconscious way. You can see this in operation when you talk with someone in a down mood and you suddenly feel depressed, or someone enthusiastic helps you to move to a happier state. Just being in the room with people who seem addicted to negativity can make you feel down.

Researchers have labeled this phenomenon the *chain damping effect,* which occurs when a person dumps a string of problems on one person and then another until anyone who listens becomes downcast. The result is mental and emotional fatigue. In sharp contrast are the leaders who understand the contagion value of enthusiasm. They spread positive emotions of upbeat attitude, resilience, and adaptability until anyone who listens becomes proactive and ready to charge.

Daniel Goleman, in his book *Primal Leadership*, studied several hundred companies and found that those with a positively charged work environment demonstrate reduced turnover, increased customer satisfaction and superior profits.

Many outstanding business leaders in the twentieth century have been able to extend their influence by radiating a positive feeling in the business environment, which results from a combination of shared purpose and emotional intelligence. They lead by telling stories. Others sense and respond to the power of these stories. These leaders are sensitive to nonverbal cues in their storytelling including their voice tone, gestures, facial expressions, and other small details.

In their book *Resonant Leadership*, Richard Boyatsis and Annie McKee point out that leaders who create resonance are those who intuitively understand or have developed the competencies of emotional intelligence. Aware of their feelings and empathic about the feelings of others, they act with mental clarity. They are able to manage stress and avoid the burnout that undercuts their ability to be fully engaged in the workplace.

How Do You Resonate?

Most people read the nonverbal signals. Some, however, are more aware of this emotional information than others. Those who do not read resonance well usually appear to me in two different ways.

The first group includes people who appear indifferent to other people's feelings. They are often uncommunicative and seem to be unwilling to communicate what is really on their minds. They may be shy; however that isn't always the case. They are often simply private people, who prefer using analytical skills and have not developed the people-reading skills to constantly interpret emotional information. The good news is these people can develop resonance management skills with practice.

The second group who do not read resonance well includes a group of people who are extremely feeling sensitive and have the natural potential for people reading. Their problem comes from being overly sensitive to *their own* feelings. Not paying attention to using their thinking and feeling skills in a balanced way, they overprocess their feelings. When this happens, they start to project their feelings onto other people, rather than reading the other person's feelings independently.

Notice that both groups of people have a common problem. They are not using both the analytical and emotional sides of their brains in an integrated way. As a result, they are handicapped in accurately understanding the resonance they both give and receive.

Those who were educated prior to the past 10 years probably were never introduced to skills of emotional intelligence in school. While schools talked about educating the whole child, most schools gave preference to cognitive skill development. However, with the advance of brain research, educators now increasingly realize the importance of training both sides of the brain.

Tuning one's radar to understand nonverbal cues is an important skill for building relationships. If you have a blind spot in recognizing nonverbal communication and processing emotional information, you need to develop these skills. Here's a plan that can help you.

Your Clear Sight Plan

1. Seek opportunities to meet people in informal ways to get to know them.
2. Ask questions that help you understand people's feelings and motivation.
3. Incorporate stories with emotional impact into your conversations to create an engaging environment that is motivational to others.

You may feel awkward at first as you begin to implement these activities. Stay with them and within a few weeks they will become more natural for you.

Seek Informal Ways to Get to Know People

Getting to know people outside the shared commentary on projects and deadlines is important. If you haven't done this before, try taking 15 minutes at the start and middle of each day to walk around and run into people just for quick two-minute chats. This will allow you to thank people for a job well done or ask them about how things are going personally. Nothing serious need be discussed. Just create an opportunity to appear friendly and interested in others. While at first this may seemed contrived if you've never done it, after awhile it becomes natural. You may even look forward to these breaks as a chance to relax.

Schedule regular, informal, individual lunches with people who are involved in some aspect of your work to get to know them better. Lunch provides time to get acquainted without discussing specific projects or assignments. It enables you to build relationships where you have a comfort level in picking up the phone anytime to talk informally about issues of mutual concern.

Make the effort to work with several new people whose styles are different from your own. They will be able to provide you with a different point of view. All of these approaches give you time to ask questions to understand people's feelings and motivations toward their work.

If you are someone who is recognized only as providing negative feedback, adopt the approach of the balanced scorecard in reviewing projects with people. Ask about what is going right, and then what needs improvement. Give feedback in the same way, always starting with something positive and then identifying any concerns. This will give you a chance to present a more balanced picture of yourself, providing both praise and criticism. You will also be able to observe how praise and criticism appear to affect other people's motivation.

Incorporate Stories with Emotional Impact

Storytelling is a wonderful way to build resonance because stories are vehicles that convey emotional information easily.

Begin to look for personal stories about your own life that convey motivation toward positive outcomes. Weave these stories into your conversations to provide an upbeat tone for what you are discussing. The goal is to convey impressions that will stimulate both the analytical and emotional brains of your audience.

Storytelling can also be a restful break in everyone's serious conversation. It provides ways to gauge how stressed people you work with are feeling. When people are really worn and exhausted, stories can help them to become calmer and quieter. This provides a more constructive environment for discussing difficult issues.

Observe the people who are particularly concerned about how decisions affect people. Make it a point to ask these individuals how they feel about something under consideration. In this way, you express not only concern for their feelings, but learn information about strengths and vulnerabilities of projects that you may not have thought about previously.

As you begin to implement these activities, you may feel awkward about trying to build skills in these soft, emotional areas. Once you start your walk-around visits and storytelling, you will find that you have the skills to make these new approaches work. You just haven't done them before.

As you experience people with different styles from your own and begin to understand their differing motivations, you will develop your own radar tuning abilities. You will find that you increase your own motivation in the process and may even find yourself personally mentoring others to learn these lessons.

Connecting Energy, Strength, and Resonance

As we discussed in Chapter 13, the busyness of business life can strongly impact our stress levels and in turn how effectively we use our strengths. This ultimately influences how well we transmit and receive resonance. In essence, the greater our tension and lower our energy, the more we do not have our receptors available to process emotional information and its resonance. This decreases productivity, judgment, and ultimately our successes.

Robert Thayer, a professor at California State University, identified four different energy states, two of which can diminish our ability to draw upon our strengths.

The two strength-sapping states are called *tense-energy* and *tense-tired*. When feeling tense-energy, you are feeling excited and powerful and push yourself to achieve goals. However, your ability to attend to your own and other's needs and projects is diminished, and burnout can result. In contrast, when feeling tense-tired you are exhausted and burned out, yet unable to gain relaxation or sleep. It may lead to restless sleep or even depression if sustained.

The two strength-building states are *calm-energy* and *calm-tired*. When feeling calm-energy, we feel serene and at peace. It is a state in which we can easily shift to neutral and make choices about how we use our strengths. We experience it too infrequently in our busyness, which is unfortunate because in this state we are able to do a lot more without feeling tense. Calm-tired is a pleasant state of winding down from challenging assignments. Your mind is free from the tension and problems you have faced.

Being calm and energized is the most open state for being aware of the effects of your resonance. You will also be better attuned to others. It is also the state in which you are best able to recognize your blind spots and make choices about how to use your strengths.

How Do *You* Resonate?

Do you understand the type of resonance you set in motion by your presence and way of communicating? How do you experience the resonance of others?

Resonance exists within us. It is an emotion, or energy, that we create for ourselves. As we've seen in using the Confidence Triangle, it is the resonance of our feelings that gives energy to our strengths. It gives commitment to our values. This unique emotional tone we experience in ourselves gives us presence.

Before moving on to Chapter 15, think about your resonance. It may be strong and explosive or quiet and calming. What state is it in most of the time? However you experience it, describe in a few words or sentences the presence you believe others experience in relating to you. What is the power of that experience? Note your reactions as part of your personal self-portrait.

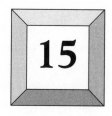

Connect

WHILE RESONANCE HELPS us to establish our presence with others, connection engages us in relationships. Rosamund and Benjamin Zander in their book *The Art of Possibility* discuss the practice of *enrollment* as "the art and practice of generating a spark of possibility for others to share." When we ignite this spark, we are able to build relationships in ways that engage others to participate. We are inspired to utilize our strengths for shared purpose and do not doubt that others are ready to join our efforts.

Sometimes, however, we fall into communicating not the world of possibilities, but the world of restrictions. This blind spot leads us to perceive limitations in ourselves and other people. We are unable to connect with others with trust, and may inaccurately perceive our own and other people's intentions.

- We communicate too loudly or too softly for others to hear us.
- We keep talking and stop listening when we feel stressed, or we withdraw and don't talk enough.
- We seem unapproachable to other people.
- We talk at people rather than engaging them in conversation.
- We see resistance in others to our ideas and potential that may not really exist.

- We don't acknowledge the contribution of others and see only our own needs.
- We retreat from opportunities to meet new people who could appreciate our strengths and create new possibilities for us.

Working from these blind spots, we limit ourselves, our relationships, our network of acquaintances, and our ability to connect with each of these groups.

In contrast, connection creates the interaction that helps build relationships. This could be a boss talking to members of his team about their goals, an individual reaching out to peers on a shared project, or someone trying to build a network to find a job. It can involve a lengthy discussion on a subject of some complexity or a brief interaction about a simple topic. Connection is more than just information sharing. It is the act of bringing our selves to our interactions.

Blind spots create the attitudes, feelings, and behaviors that block our ability to connect with other people. To connect, we need to be able to bring ourselves into the present moment. Blind spots can keep us in a state of physical stress, detachment, or entrapment by our feelings, and ignorant of the possibilities of our thoughts.

When we connect we gain the clear sight needed to relate to someone else in a meaningful way. It does not necessarily mean we are always in agreement or that we leave every discussion with a shared purpose. However, we will have listened to one another's point of view without judgment and provided our point of view.

My work with Warren helped me to understand the meaning of connection. He was a man who understood how to connect with others.

Engaging Warren

When I think about my experience of connection with leaders, I remember Warren, CEO of a financial services company. At 50, he had been with his company for 30 years and had worked his way up from his start as a salesperson. He had built his business strategy through hands-on experience in businesses he had run. His company's performance was top-of-the pack.

Warren was an engaging man. He had an energy that comes from being totally dedicated to what he was doing. Interested in the people who were a part of his business, he made a commitment to developing them. When I walked around the company with Warren, he made an effort to talk to people at all different levels of the organization. He was aware of small details about their work and lives.

When I conversed with Warren about a business issue, he listened carefully and shared his perspective. He made me feel my observations were important. He was very clear about what he supported and didn't support. Warren demonstrated the qualities of connection:

- *Appears approachable.* He appears mentally and emotionally present, and conveys a sense of shared purpose. He is at ease with himself and seems trustworthy.
- *Engages in discussion.* He conveys information clearly, listens to what I say, and encourages open discussion of problems and concerns. He presents ideas convincingly and provides clear feedback.
- *Recognizes the contributions of others.* He encourages discussion of what I did right or wrong, shares credit, and communicates an understanding of my value.
- *Acknowledges differences of opinion without judgment.* He recognizes where views differ, will change his mind if presented with convincing information, attempts to resolve conflicts but is clear about when his opinion will prevail.
- *Socially savvy.* He knows many people well and builds access to a network of people. He values others regardless of their status. He takes accountability for mistakes.

Warren was a man who chose his words very carefully. Don Miquel Ruiz, in his article "Speak With Impeccability," points out that successful people are the masters of their words, as they are conscious of what they think and speak. They carefully choose words that build relationships and dreams. When we are conscious of our words, we speak from a place of intention and integrity.

A meeting with Warren left me feeling positive and motivated. Of course, no one is perfect, and he had his bad days and stressful moments. But on a consistent basis, the experience I had of meeting with Warren is that he was a balanced, open, trustworthy man who valued my contributions and respected my thinking. He is someone I made a connection with.

Characteristics of Disconnection

When we develop blind spots, we lose sight not only of our words and their impact on others, but of the overall nature of our relationships. With diminished connection to one another, we all lose out in the process. This disconnection results when we:

- *Appear unapproachable.* Seeming unapproachable, untrustworthy, or uncomfortable with other people, we make others feel we aren't interested in what they have to say.
- *Disengage.* Not speaking clearly, not listening to what others have to say, not providing useful feedback, we may not present our ideas convincingly.
- *Ignore the contributions of others.* Taking credit for what others do, we don't communicate how we value what they do and get lost in our own agendas.
- *Act judgmentally or create conflict.* Judging other people or igniting issues that create ill will lead to conflict and disconnection.
- *Lack social skills.* Not reaching out to people because they are junior to us, or not taking the time to understand others, shifting blame: These behaviors destroy relationships.

Sometimes we choose to limit our connections with other people; we may not have the time or resources to engage. However, many people are *unable* to connect because their view of themselves or other peo-ple is clouded.

Identifying Your Disconnectors

The Blind Spot 360 can be very helpful to you in identifying where you may be losing connection. Once you see the specific behaviors needed to be improved, you can easily develop a clear sight plan in response to that behavior.

For example, Michael was senior program leader of an engineering team with 15 years of experience and respect for his knowledge and expertise. However, his team found him unapproachable, because he was constantly judging their shortcomings. He felt it was his responsi-bility to maintain high standards, and insure that things were done the right way. The team believed Michael used the high standards mantra as a way to limit and devalue the many contributions they were making so he could always be seen as the most knowledgeable person on the team.

Michael was disconnecting from his team by ignoring three of the characteristics of connection: (1) he appeared unapproachable; (2) he ignored the contributions of members of his team; and (3) he acted judg-mentally in communication with junior members of the team.

Michael could begin connecting with his team by focusing on these three behaviors.

You will be able to identify your disconnectors as Michael did through the Blind Spot 360. Once identified, develop your clear sight plan to address the targeted behavior.

Sometimes, your disconnection from someone else may not be your fault. The other person may be the source of the disconnection. How-ever, to get reconnected you may want to take the lead. This was the case with Cathy, whose boss was carrying so much stress that he was in a constant state of disconnection from her. Cathy considered his problem her problem and worked to lift the stresses that were causing the discon-nection. The results were positive for both Cathy and her boss, as you will see.

Cathy Helps Her Boss to Reconnect

Cathy was goal-oriented, managed stress without feeling it, and enjoyed the social interaction of the workplace. Warm, friendly, outgoing, and enthusiastic when you met her, Cathy liked to have fun at work. As the head of a design team for a major architectural firm, she supervised 10 people and reported to one of the senior partners. Creative and attracted to the innovative thinking that went on in the firm, she also liked the competition and results orientation. I worked with Cathy when she decided to improve communication with her boss.

So what was the connection problem for Cathy? She reported to a serious boss, who was uncomfortable with her management style. He was very detail-oriented and liked to be on top of any changes going on in major projects at all times. The boss saw Cathy's go-with-the-flow style as a little too relaxed for his comfort level. He kept calling her for information and seemed stressed by not knowing about minor changes in projects. The tone of his voice made Cathy stop and take time to figure out what was going on. She asked me to help her understand what might not be working.

To get a better idea of why her boss seemed edgy around her, Cathy asked him to do the Blind Spot 360 on her. The results gave her a good opportunity to have a frank and candid discussion about what was not working for him.

Boss Often Sees in Cathy

- At ease with herself.
- Resolves conflicts.
- Knows many people well.

Boss Seldom Sees in Cathy

- Conveys information clearly.
- Listens to what I say.

- Welcomes both positive and negative feedback.
- Encourages open discussion about projects and concerns.

From this information and their discussion, Cathy realized that her boss didn't think he was getting enough information about what was going on. He felt she wasn't giving him enough of the bad news. His constant checking back with her on details had initially made Cathy feel that she wasn't trusted. She had felt micromanaged. Now she began to understand that he was constantly asking for information because others asked it of him. That's what he needed to feel on top of things. It wasn't that he blamed her for what went wrong. He just didn't feel he could do his job well without knowing what wasn't working at all times.

Cathy didn't take this feedback personally after she had thought about it. She needed to destress by running four miles, but she was quickly able to shift to neutral by trying to see the world from his point of view. Here's a copy of Cathy's Clear Sight Plan.

Cathy's Clear Sight Plan

Goal: To strengthen my connection and working relationship with my boss.

1. Develop a briefing system that can keep my boss up-to-the-minute on what is happening on all our projects.
2. Increase the breadth of issues we cover in our regular meetings so that I can be involved in all the cutting edge new projects that are on the firm's horizon.

In implementing the plan, Cathy set up a briefing system to give her boss very detailed daily updates on her team's projects, particularly potential pitfalls—many of which never led to problems. It was a bit of a nuisance to do this red alert report, but she thought that it would be exactly what he needed to do his job.

The system had a dramatic effect in lowering her boss's stress.

With this daily status report in place, Cathy found that other meetings with him could deal with broader issues. He was appreciative of her project control, and was willing to bring her into other projects.

They were able to connect more genuinely in meetings. He began to engage Cathy in the early stages of new projects that were on the cutting edge of the firm's growth. The openness of their communication sparked creativity for them and spirited some interesting new strategic directions for the firm. Cathy grew personally and professionally and was able to take on increasingly important assignments.

Expanding the Network

The word *network* has become so overused that it conjures horrific images of people glad-handing others to reach their goals. Keith Ferrazzi, in his book *Never Eat Alone*, provides a more natural and personal approach to genuine relationship building based on generosity and the ability to connect friends with friends. Expanding your relationships is about what other people want as well as what you want. You need to reach out to others not just when you need something, but on a regular basis if you want to develop a true sense of connection.

If you're someone who feels awkward about putting yourself out there with new people, you might begin with a simple exercise I suggest to clients with similar feelings, who are usually new members of a seasoned team; If you are nervous about opening your mouth for the first time in a group meeting, develop a clear sight plan to take small steps. You can establish your presence in a meeting by planning in advance to make a comment at a preprogrammed time in the meeting, say at 12 minutes into a meeting and then again at 40 minutes into the meeting.

What you say isn't as important as simply expressing something so people know you are there. You could simply build on the point of whoever the last speaker was, such as, "I'd like to talk about that with my team. . . . We have a similar situation. . . . How do you suggest I raise it for the first time?" The point is to start becoming visible.

While this approach may sound silly to you, it usually works. It starts you speaking up.

Rather than sitting and watching, you begin engaging. Two to three observations raised each meeting will increase your comfort level with this group. Too many of us hold off talking because we feel pressure to say something brilliant. That expectation only creates more tension. Your goal is just to raise your voice.

Another thing to do is to set up informal sessions with various team members to get to know them and what they expected from you. Comfortable conversations in the hallway or on the phone can help to make you feel like an insider. You'll begin to feel more comfortable with your group.

If you feel awkward about getting conversations going in situations where you know no one, I recommend Debra Fine's book *The Fine Art of Small Talk*. It's a wonderful primer on how to feel comfortable in any situation. She provides list of conversation starters that can get you moving anywhere.

Broaden the Network

Broaden your network by having informal meetings with others throughout the organization. Some will be senior to you. Others may be peers. All people who are connected in some way to your work or work product can be lunch partners. Such meetings can run a half hour to an hour and don't have a task-oriented agenda, just an opportunity to try to understand what the other person is doing and to share some ideas. These meetings are important to building relationships and connecting.

Such lunches can lead to phone conversations about a variety of issues. You can e-mail information you think might be useful to another person. Try to introduce people you meet to other people you think would have something to share. You will find yourself included in gatherings and parties that others are holding.

Career Building

Slowly you may find that you are actually enjoying this process of meeting new people and sharing ideas. When you start thinking about new career options for yourself, expand your network to meet with others inside and outside the organization, who can give you new insights.

When searching for a new job outside your organization, work to find new contacts who can connect you with people who have connections to companies where you want to interview. This is hard work. You have to focus your intentions clearly on what you want to learn about and how to find a link to someone who could serve as a resource.

Appreciating the help other people have given to you, always be available to help other people. This give-and-take is the rhythm of these relationships. Following these behaviors will slowly establish you as a very likeable individual.

The Importance of Likeability

Author Tim Sanders' book *The Likeability Factor* identifies a number of interesting pieces of research that support his thesis that likeability, the ability to create positive attitudes in other people, is important to our success. For example, a study at Columbia University by Melinda Tamkins showed that popular workers received faster promotions and raises and were perceived as more trustworthy. A 2,000-person study at Yale concluded that the most successful leaders were not aggressive but likeable and respectful of their employees.

Sanders sees your likeability determined by four factors: (1) friendliness, the ability to communicate openness to others; (2) relevance, the capacity to connect with others' interests, wants, and needs; (3) empathy, the ability to recognize and acknowledge others' feelings; and (4) the integrity and authenticity with which you express your likeability.

You do not need to be likeable to connect with others, but being likeable often makes connecting far easier.

Think about your own strengths and blind spots related to connection. You can go back to the model of Warren to gain perspective. Make a note of what you need to work on for the personal self-portrait you are developing.

With an idea of how well you connect to others, you are ready for Section Five, where you can view *their* blind spots.

Section Five

See Their Blind Spots

We've focused on seeing our own blind spots and understanding how they affect our goals and relationships. Now it's time to focus on the blind spots of others who are affecting us. How can we understand *their* core strengths and blind spots in ways that help us to meet our goals?

Chapter 16: See *Their* Way

View the blind spots of your boss and significant others in ways that can help you to understand the dynamics underlying your relationships.

- What is their *Blind Spots Profile*?

Chapter 17: Identify Group Blind Spots

You sometimes participate in a group where you represent a minority view on any number of dimensions—cultural, gender, thinking style, religion, ethnicity, age, sexual orientation, disability, economic status.

- Complete the *Group Blind Spots Finder* to identify any group biases that might influence how you think and feel about yourself, and how you think others think and feel about you.

16

See *Their* Way

WE'VE BEEN FOCUSING on *your* strengths and blind spots. Others viewing you have strengths and blind spots of their own. So what happens when their blind spots meet your blind spots? Be guided by the third principle of clear sight, Simply Focus on Success. What do you need to know about others' blind spots that are important to achieving your success?

A few observations about other people's blind spots are:

- Their blind spots may distort the perception of who they think you are; they see you through the lens of how they see the world.
- People similar to you in style, personality, and traits may see the world in ways similar to your own.
- People dissimilar to you in style, personality and traits may need more explanation about your actions, if they are to accurately understand your intentions.
- Sometimes, people can be using the same words yet have totally different understandings of the topic they are discussing.

These observations about other people's blind spots apply to groups as well. Groups of people acting together form a culture, which has strengths and blind spots of its own. By understanding the strengths and potential blind spots of a culture, we can better manage the blind spots we have in relating to the members of the cultural group.

Blind Spots in Individuals

To relate this to a real situation, let's go back and revisit Joey, the entertaining salesperson in Chapter 1, who missed promotion to sales manager. This time rather than focusing on Joey, let's explore how Joey's boss, Hector was influenced by blind spots in his relationship to Joey.

Clearly, Joey hadn't spent much time thinking about Hector until he missed his promotion. Then Joey suddenly realized that his understanding of Hector was important. What could Joey have learned just from observing Hector?

Hector was a soft-spoken man who was never demonstrative about his feelings or expectations. He presented his thoughts factually and straightforwardly. While cordial, he never seemed to express any emotion about anything. He was a man of few words unless he became very interested in a subject that he could talk about for a long time. He was interested in sales strategy and focused on structuring the commission plan. He dressed conservatively and spent much of his time alone. Hector's boss seemed to rely on him heavily to analyze company sales strategies. While Hector went on sales calls when required, he didn't seem to enjoy them. He delegated sales responsibilities whenever possible.

Hector was a careful, thoughtful man. Joey should have been able to figure out that when Hector said something was important he meant it. The reason Joey missed the importance of Hector's warning about sales reports and meetings was because he simply hadn't been paying attention.

Putting the Clues Together

Where might Hector's blind spots lie and how would they appear to Joey? We can speculate by thinking through which Blind Spots Profile would apply to Hector. Our guess may be incorrect. However, just by giving attention to this thought process, Joey can develop insights to help him better understand Hector's worldview.

Hector appears too reserved to be extroverted in feeling style. He seems more introspective or interpersonal. He also doesn't appear to be focused on feelings or image of others, so he probably is not a Feelings First thinker. Reading over the possible personal models in the Appendix Blind Spots Profile Matrix, we look at the four styles in the Introspective and Interpersonal rows, and the Read Ideas First and Read Instincts First columns. Two categories seem to fit Hector best: the Responsible High-Standards Builder and the Reserved Analytical Strategist, which are summarized in the following illustration.

Reviewing these models, we see that either model describes a person who takes his thoughts seriously. "Self-discipline" and "methodical" describe a person whose words are carefully selected. It is important to listen to their suggestions. They would probably take note of someone who doesn't follow through on a suggestion they said was important. Perhaps Hector had told Joey about sales reports and meetings several times, and Joey missed this cue because he wasn't attuned to how Hector operates. How would Hector's blind spots show up? Well, both models suggest someone who becomes distant and aloof when blinded. Perhaps, when

---

RESPONSIBLE HIGH-STANDARDS BUILDER

Greatest Personal Strength: Innate self-discipline and standards for doing the right thing for the organization.

Potential Blind Spot: In pursuit of goals can become too serious and overly responsible. Can become distant, angry, aloof, and inflexible when too focused.

RESERVED ANALYTICAL STRATEGIST

Greatest Personal Strength: Insightful methodical ability to see both forest and trees.

Potential Blind Spot: Can move too much into the head and become distant and aloof. When pressed can become distracted and dictatorial.

Which Model Describes Hector Better?

Joey had ignored Hector's suggestion for sales reports and meeting attendance, Hector just withdrew. If Joey hadn't taken the time to notice this, he might have just continued to focus on what he, rather than Hector, felt was important.

So how would these two men's blind spots interact? Joey loves the interaction of sales calls and is attentive to feelings and image. Hector reserves his feelings and expresses his attention methodically and deliberately. When operating from a blind spot, Hector might give up on Joey, and then withdraw and ignore him. Joey in contrast accelerates and gets distracted when operating from his blind spot. He keeps making sales calls constantly even when they interfere with Hector's requirements. Joey totally missed Hector's silent withdrawal reaction and just assumed Hector's suggestion wasn't important. How did this scenario affect Joey's promotion? We'll never know for sure, but these are the situations that play out behind the scenes with great influence on events.

Perspective

This whole thought process took us about five minutes to mull over. Granted if you haven't done it before, it may seem a bit confusing at first. As you work with the models identified in the Blind Spots Profile Matrix, you will want to rename them for people you know. For example, Joey was so excited about the system that he got Hector to identify a personal model for himself, which *was* the Reserved Analytical Strategist. Joey has renamed that model, the Hector Model, which helps him to remember it more easily. Joey was beginning to understand Hector's strengths and blind spots. Putting effort into understanding the worldviews of people we deal with every day is a worthwhile investment in our success.

Blind Spots in Organizations and Groups

Now let's further imagine that Joey works for an organization where the dominant style of thinking and feeling of the culture resembles that of Hector. This would be a Reserved Analytical Strategist culture, or what

Joey now calls The Hector Crowd. This culture is thoughtful and precise about their work. They are independent people who like to consider assignments carefully before they discuss them. They wouldn't like others coming at them emotionally, but prefer logical, principled discussion of projects. Innovative strategies and fairness in compensation and rewards are highly regarded principles.

How would Joey operate successfully within this culture? First, he needs to realize that he is in the minority position. Others are not going to naturally understand his views. He will probably be more outgoing and focused on feeling and image than others around him. He may find meetings with others to be slow and too analytical for his tastes. He would prefer more energy and excitement. If he allows himself to feel like an outsider, he could become isolated. However, if Joey recognizes his uniqueness and communicates his value to others, he may be perceived as a big asset. Joey likes lots of interaction and dealing with customers, and he does it well. Others will probably be very happy to have someone they feel confident in to handle this part of the business. Joey will have the best shot at being valued by the culture at large when he takes responsibility for communicating that value to others.

Seeing It Their Way

Joey can guide his exploration of this culture by following the principles of clear sight. If Joey recognizes the natural strengths of this organization and the style and rules by which it operates, he will be able to approach it with an open mind. Following the first principle of clear sight, he will be able to Shift to Neutral.

Following the third principle of clear sight, Joey will Simply Focus on Success. He will recognize how his differences can be valued by the majority culture and communicate that benefit to the group so they see how effectively he works with them.

Working within a culture different from one's own takes work. Joey will need to follow the fourth principle of clear sight, Stretch Your Strengths. If the culture at large talks the language of finance and discipline, Joey will need to learn their language while simultaneously helping them to appreciate his primary language of sales.

The fifth principle of Choose with Confidence will help Joey to appreciate how to keep a balance between recognizing his own strengths and responding to the needs and strengths of the culture at large.

Different Cultural Worlds

We live in an international world, where differences between countries and culture can be far more pronounced than those between Joey and Hector. Trying to understand the worldview of a company in a different culture takes careful attention.

Tanya was planning to take an assignment for a U.S. company in Saudi Arabia and had taken some training to prepare herself for her initial contacts with Saudi people. Usually an expressive, articulate woman, Tanya was feeling unsure of how she would be able to connect with other Saudis: "In the United States we value individualism, independence, self-reliance, and change. The Saudi culture values order, tradition, modesty, sacrifice, and keeping things the same. I'm not sure how we can communicate about common issues."

A good rule of thumb in this situation is to watch, listen, and learn. Tanya will be appreciated for her respect. It's also important to remember that the emotional brain is at work when one is dealing with someone in another culture. The emotional brain is testing for trustworthiness, reliability, and safety in dealing with another person. Our emotional brains communicate. It is a transcultural ability.

Sometimes wide cultural gaps are simpler to bridge than narrow ones. I remember feeling somewhat anxious as I prepared to lead a symposium for executives from the Middle East. I was a seven-months-pregnant woman, and was not sure how I would be perceived in a leadership role by Middle Eastern men. I was put at ease over lunch as one of the executives from Saudi Arabia asked how I would manage being a working mother. He was approaching me with the understanding of a woman's role in the United States, which was clear to both of us. He related to me in my institutional role, not as a woman.

Different Cultures Within an Organization

Sometimes cultural differences within an U.S.-based corporation can be more difficult to deal with than those of international differences. One example is the cross-organizational success story of the redesign of the 1995 Lincoln Continental. Their challenge was to redesign a better car in a culture that had been defined by traditional, hierarchical, authority-based values. A cultural divide existed between those in charge of producing the new model and those responsible to control costs—cultures separated by different training, professional orientation, and values.

The tension between the two groups was great from the leadership level on down. What was holding both groups back from learning to work together was getting stuck in blind spots of mistrust, fear, and resentment. Clear sight strategies involved increasing emotional awareness skills such as empathy to listen to another's perspective with sensitivity. People were taught to become aware of but not articulate their hidden thoughts and feelings about others. For example, when a member of one group yawned, the opposing group could interpret that behavior as a sign of boredom rather than the reality that the individual was tired from a late night at work. These inner dialogues reveal how people really think and feel about what is happening around them. But if we don't take the time to be aware of them, we return to operating from our blind spots.

Bosses from both production and cost control were trained as facilitators and coaches to help their teams to learn to be interconnected. These leaders were no longer controllers and generals, but had to exhibit skills in listening and empowering their people.

The end of the story demonstrated a concrete payoff as the teams learned to work together, exchange ideas, share budgets, and work as an integrated unit. The project finished way ahead of budget, ahead of schedule, and with quality.

What Are Your Differences?

Within the scope of this book, it is not my intention to provide counsel on how to manage or change cultures. I am focused on helping individuals recognize their blind spots and reach their goals. However, recognizing others people's blind spots is often an important perspective for understanding our own.

Think for a moment about a group of people you work with which may have different values, thinking, or learning styles from yours. What strengths and blind spots do they have? How can you use your strengths in a complementary way?

In Chapter 17, I introduce you to Gloria, a woman who is facing the blind spots of her family members as she tries to take charge of the family business.

17

Identify Group Blind Spots

WE MAY TRIGGER blind spots within a group, particularly when we represent a difference. Group views may be influenced by an issue of culture, gender, race, religion, ethnicity, disability, age, or economic status. They could also result from a different style of thinking or learning. Whatever the source, blind spots often result from beliefs held by one individual or group about another individual or group. This is a complicated landscape and one where it is dangerous to generalize.

To help navigate these complicated relationships, we develop a simple perspective for interacting with a group whose culture, demographics, values, beliefs, or ways of thinking may be very different from our own. Specifically, what are some of the group blind spots that can affect your confidence and effectiveness in group relationships, and how can you best see them and manage them as you pursue your goals?

Some observations to start are:

- Differences in culture, demographics, values, beliefs, and ways of thinking can create blind spots.
- When we ignore or become overly sensitive to individual differences, we may develop blind spots that hinder the group's ability to work together.

- Members of the group who represent the majority perspective may overestimate or underestimate the tensions a minority group member experiences.
- Minority group members may find it useful to test whether tensions they feel come from their visible differences or from blind spots that they may not be aware of.

To explore any blind spots a group may have that would influence you in reaching your goal, I suggest you answer the Group Blind Spots Finder. It can help you to pinpoint your concerns about the blind spots of a group you are dealing with.

The importance of this exercise is to make the feelings underlying these potential blind spots concrete. You may never confirm what the group's blind spots really are; however, you will act upon your assumptions of blind spots. This may cause you to see obstacles that aren't really there, or to underestimate obstacles that you can't immediately see.

Group Blind Spots Finder

1. In which of the following areas, if any, do you feel the group may have beliefs or blind spots that could affect you in reaching your goals with this group? Check the appropriate boxes.

   _____ culture   _____ style of thinking or learning
   _____ gender   _____ race
   _____ religion   _____ ethnicity
   _____ disability   _____ age
   _____ economic status   _____ sexual orientation

2. What belief(s) do you feel the majority of the group members hold that could influence your effectiveness in reaching your goal?

3. How would this belief specifically influence or limit your effectiveness?

4. What specific steps can you take to increase your possibilities for success?

Let's see how Gloria uses this approach in trying to step up to lead her family's business.

Gloria Assumes Control

Gloria, age 45 was the youngest child and only daughter of the Torres family. She had moved away from her family when she married and had four children. Now divorced and having completed her MBA, she had distinguished herself as an entrepreneur with a track record of building businesses.

Gloria's father, John Torres, age 85, had built the Torres Manufacturing Company to be a highly profitable enterprise. The business supported his wife and four children in a very elegant lifestyle. Sons Michael, age 52; Richard, 48; and Connor, 47 were working in the company.

When John had suddenly died from a heart attack, family cultural tradition suggested that the oldest son, Michael, would take over the company. Michael had been running the company after his father's death until a serious automobile accident left him hospitalized and disabled. While Richard had temporarily taken his brother's place as president, neither Richard nor Connor demonstrated any talent or interest in running a business. Over a couple of years, the business was declining.

I worked with Gloria as she decided what to do about the business.

Gloria decided to return to step up and try to save the family business. She deeply valued the business her father had built and saw herself as a strong, instinctive manager with a demonstrated business track record of performance. Her brothers agreed to her suggestion and her mother didn't say no. Gloria decided to try the position of president for a nine-month trial.

During her transition, Gloria sought my help to manage any problems related to blind spots that might hold her back from effectively managing the business turnaround.

Her greatest concern was whether her family, which held deep cultural beliefs about the role of the male as head of the household and business, would really support her to take over. She wanted to know what blind spots might get in her way.

She completed the Group Blind Spots Finder to pinpoint her concerns. (See the box on page 191.)

Gloria believed that her family's gender-limiting beliefs could interfere with her success as president of the company. The gender issues she identified had remained unspoken for many years. Gloria had never raised them directly with family members. She assumed these beliefs existed from behaviors she had observed as a child: While her brothers were praised for their grades and athletic achievements, she was praised for how pretty she was and how well she dressed, not for her school accomplishments. She now believed that if gender limiting beliefs were going to affect her chances for saving the company, she needed to discuss them with other family members. However, the possibility of doing this felt very uncomfortable to her.

She was ready to develop her Clear Sight Plan that follows. Her success goal was to get real support for her leadership of the company from her mother and brothers.

Gloria's Plan for Clear Sight

1. Discuss my plan for the company with each family member separately, directly asking for their support and expressing my concerns that gender may be seen as limiting my potential for the presidency.
2. Discuss with each family member my qualifications for the presidency and identify any concerns they have about me personally that could limit my success.
3. Set a plan for the results I plan to achieve in nine months, at which time I would want to be named the long-term president of the company.

As she began to implement her clear sight plan, Gloria met with each member of her family, asking for his or her support. She brought up her concern about the family cultural tradition of the male as head, the

Group Blind Spots Finder
for Gloria Torres

1. In which of the following areas, if any, do you feel the group you are dealing with may have blind spots that could influence your effectiveness with this group? Check the appropriate boxes

   _X_ culture   ____ style of thinking or learning

   _X_ gender   ____ race

   ___ religion   ____ ethnicity

   ___ disability   ____ age

   ___ economic status   ____ sexual orientation

2. What belief(s) do you feel the majority of the group members hold that could influence your effectiveness in reaching your goal?

   "My family holds traditional beliefs that the male is head of the household and business and the female takes care of the home and raises the children. The lives of my parents and brothers have followed this pattern. I question whether they will ever give me full responsibility to run the family business in spite of its current state of almost bankruptcy."

3. How would this belief specifically influence or limit your effectiveness?

   "I wonder if they will really back me up. I need them at least not to undercut my efforts. In the past I have found they were really passive aggressive. They nod assurance but don't really want me to succeed. In school, for example, my brother's accomplishments were praised and mine weren't. I was admired for how pretty I was."

4. What specific steps can you take to increase your possibilities for success?

   "I want to do everything I can to increase the chances of my success. I don't want to think negatively about my chances for turning around the business. I will look at whatever blind spots exist that could negatively influence my chances."

female as supporter. It was awkward at first for Gloria to discuss these issues, since for so many years they had been unspoken.

Her three brothers expressed more concern over whether the business would be run effectively. They were able to separate their own personal practice of having nonworking wives from the business role their sister would play in the company. They had seen her track record in business and were comfortable with her business sense. However, they had some concern over whether Gloria would be able to deal with them without getting too pushy sometimes. After all, they owned the company, too, and wanted to have their ideas heard. Gloria agreed to work on this.

The conversation with Gloria's mother Eva was a little more difficult. Eva still believed that one of the brothers should be president, like her husband had been. She said she respected Gloria's talent, but was old-fashioned and wasn't quite comfortable with Gloria running things. She said she would try to keep an open mind.

Gloria wasn't sure how her mother really felt. She thought part of Eva's feelings was cultural and part was related to unconscious jealousy that Gloria was getting a chance that Eva never had. Gloria would keep talking with her mother throughout the coming months to keep their communication open. They had never had a bad relationship, but certainly there had been many issues never discussed between them over the years.

Gloria Identifies Her Blind Spots

Responding to her brother's comments about her pushy ways, Gloria decided to complete the Blind Spots Profile. She found these two models that described her blind spots.

In thinking about these models, Gloria observed that as a young woman she was probably a natural Assertive Get-It-Doner, who was a strong leader. She developed the Warm Relationship Builder approach because understanding the feelings and needs of other people was what she was rewarded for as a female. She recognized that the Assertive Get-It-Doner's bossiness and confrontation seemed to show through when she was stressed.

WARM RELATIONSHIP BUILDER

Greatest Personal Strength: Innate understanding of the feelings and needs of others.

Potential Blind Spot: If feelings not reciprocated appropriately, can focus on personal shortcomings and withdraw.
Can try to avoid negative feelings and become manipulative.

ASSERTIVE DIRECT GET-IT-DONER

Greatest Personal Strength: Knows how to get big things done.

Potential Blind Spot: Can become too confrontational or bossy.
When unappreciated can become suspicious and mistrustful.

Which Model Describes Gloria Better?

Gloria readily owned the blind spot of being too confrontational or bossy and recognized that it may disturb other people as her brothers had pointed out. Perhaps their push-back against her in the past had to do with her confrontational style under stress, as much as with her feelings about gender limitations.

Gloria Succeeds in Running the Business

As president Gloria was able to breathe fresh life into the company. Results started to improve in her nine months as head. She met biweekly with each of her brothers by phone or in person and was careful to listen to their input on the business—even if she chose not to follow it. Slowly, they gained confidence in her new focus and openness.

Gloria also spent time with her mother and tried to find some new ways they could relate to each other. However, Gloria found the relationship only became more uncomfortable. Eva was not interested in Gloria's successes in running the business and didn't want to discuss them. She criticized Gloria for the breakup in her marriage and reiterated that Gloria's priorities were in the wrong place. Gloria tried to focus their time together on shopping or entertaining her children.

When it came time for Gloria to take over as ongoing president, the family was split. Gloria and her brothers were in favor. Her mother was opposed but was not willing to say why. Only when her oldest son Michael asked his mother to support his decision to back Gloria did Eva agree to the decision.

Gloria and her brothers agreed on a compensation package for Gloria, which included a five-year contract. The brothers believed that their best interests were represented by having Gloria continue as president. Gloria's mother never discussed the matter again. She never said exactly why, but Gloria perceived it was the old belief that women have a place in the family at home but not running a business. Her mother never denied this, but would simply not discuss it.

The Truth Sets Gloria Free

Gloria was very pleased that she was able to open communication with her family members who revealed their true positions. She felt good about these relationships because she was clear about what she could expect. There were no longer any hidden secrets. She was grateful for her brothers' support and at peace with her mother's limitations. Gloria had opened the blind spots and had nothing left to fear: "While it's a sad fact, my mother basically was the one who held views limiting my potential as a woman, I don't resent her for it anymore. I just accept it and am grateful to leave the old ghosts behind."

In our last meeting together, Gloria reviewed how she felt about her confidence and well-being. She had been able to break through old biases that she felt her brothers held and had learned that the gender limiting views were carried by her mother, which saddened her. She also realized that some of the push-back she had felt from her brothers was probably not as much a result of their gender beliefs but more related to her bossy style. In taking over the presidency, she had a new sense of confidence that she was fully capable of running the business and that she had brought all of the blind spots out of the closet. In many ways the truth had set her free.

Discussing this in terms of the Confidence Triangle, Gloria had an accurate assessment of both her strengths as president and the professional value she was perceived to have from the family. Her feelings about her own capabilities, her brothers' support, and her mother's limited view of women were at peace. As a result she resonated with self-confidence and well-being.

The story of Gloria gives us a picture of the complexity of group beliefs and blind spots. Gloria's initial concerns about the family's biases

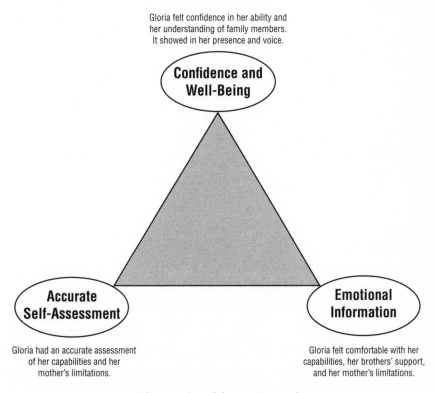

Gloria felt confidence in her ability and
her understanding of family members.
It showed in her presence and voice.

**Confidence and
Well-Being**

**Accurate
Self-Assessment**

**Emotional
Information**

Gloria had an accurate assessment
of her capabilities and her
mother's limitations.

Gloria felt comfortable with her
capabilities, her brothers' support,
and her mother's limitations.

Gloria's Confidence Triangle

were tested. She recognized the possible limitations in others' thinking but didn't allow it to diminish her dreams or actions. Realizing that she had transcended the limitations of her mother's world view made Gloria feel stronger—both for herself and her mother. She had left no unfinished business and could accept her mother's worldview without being limited by it.

Are there any groups you are dealing with where you feel you are in a minority position by gender, culture, thinking and learning style, or any of the other dimensions mentioned in the Group Blind Spots Finder?

If so, fill out the Group Blind Spots Finder, which can be found in the Appendix, as it relates to your relationship with that group. Think about how to approach that blind spot so it doesn't limit your success. Add this information to your personal self-portrait.

Aware of the limitations of group blind spots, you are ready to consider the influence time plays in helping you to discover and effectively manage your blind spots.

Section Six

Build Success
for Life

These two closing chapters provide a glimpse of how our blind spots conceal the changing purpose of our lives and the lives of others important to us.

Chapter 18: Find Purpose Over Time

The meaning of success changes as we see ourselves in different situations. Sometimes the purpose of our lives becomes clear early in life. For many people, it evolves over time and may not become clear until later in life, or as we prepare for *Second Adult Life*. Follow the steps of your changing blind spots to see how your purpose is finding you.

- Are you ready to prepare a *Statement of Purpose* for your life?

Chapter 19: Pass the Possibilities

When people begin to identify their own blind spots and get clear sight, they are thrilled by how successful and energized they feel. Often they want every person who affects their work and life to find clear sight, too. Find out how to talk to others constructively about their blind spots.

- Follow the *Five Principles of Clear Sight* to help others identify and clarify their blind spots.

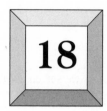

Find Purpose Over Time

THE MEANING OF SUCCESS changes over time as we get to know ourselves in new situations. As life throws us challenges, we realize the strengths that guide us through changes and setbacks. We learn what we are committed to and feel purposeful about. We see through the blind spots that hide parts of ourselves that we couldn't see before.

Most of us want to be somebody. Richard Leider, author of *The Power of Purpose*, sees our purpose as the "deepest dimension within us—our core or essence—where we have a profound sense of who we are, where we came from, and where we're going. Purpose is the quality we choose to shape our lives around. Purpose is a source of energy and direction."

We find our purpose as we develop a sense of who we *think* we are. As we *feel* our reactions to changing circumstances, we realize that who we thought we were may be different from whom we have become. Our sense of self comes largely from our values, purpose, and feelings about capabilities we have to achieve that purpose.

Recognizing blind spots is an essential part of seeing the potential for who we are and who we are becoming:

- When we are unaware of important aspects of our capabilities, our blind spots hold us back from seeing our personal potential.

- When the expectations of others continually dominate our own, we are blinded from understanding our feelings of stress, anxiety, depression, or withdrawal.
- When we lose touch with our feelings about what is important, we move into blind spots that lead us to feel purposeless.
- When we are unaware of how we affect those around us, we lose our sense of connection and feel isolated.

As we question these blind spots, we see ourselves more accurately. The more reality based we become in understanding our strengths, values, goals, and purpose, the more confidence we feel in our selves.

Viktor Frankl, a psychologist who was imprisoned in a concentration camp during World War II, observed that only in a crisis do we find the self we have actually become. In crisis, we come face-to-face with our selves. Our values are severely tested. Goals that once seemed central lose importance. We find strengths we never knew we had.

As we experience life and gain wisdom and self-knowledge, we develop a deeper understanding of our *self*. The person we know our self to be in our twenties changes into a new person within us in our thirties, forties, fifties and further throughout life. We evolve, we reevaluate the meaning of success and how we see the strengths and the blind spots that affect our actions.

Your life mission can be viewed from one perspective as a series of opportunities for understanding blind spots that emerge when we fail to recognize natural changes within ourselves. Such changes are partially a newly emerging part of your personality and partially a response to the changing circumstances of your environment. These changes that occur every 7 to 10 years create new possibilities for your life and work.

To understand the role that these blind spots play throughout your life, follow Taylor's course of self discovery over a 25-year period.

Taylor: Encouraged to Achieve

Taylor was the oldest of four children and was encouraged by both parents to achieve. This achievement orientation became a big part of her life orientation. A strong student, she also participated in many school activities, went to a name college, and graduated with a job at a major corporation's marketing department. A mover and shaker in producing results, Taylor was quickly promoted.

At the age of 26, Taylor wanted to see her career directions more clearly. She took the Blind Spots Profile, identified her primary personal model as an Optimistic Image-Oriented Producer, and recognized her gut strengths. She was indeed an achievement-oriented multitasker and loved developing many different marketing programs and projects. She also desired the positive feedback of her boss to complete her feeling of success. She loved the extroverted experience of making speeches and directing other people.

Taylor's career continued to soar. She married, had two children, and continued to follow the voice calling for more achievement. By her mid-thirties, however, Taylor felt tired and somewhat listless in spite of her constant achievement. Her blind spot of too much multitasking to support work and home life was leading her to feel more distant and alienated from others. However, she also began to hear an inner voice, a weird feeling that made her think about changes in her life. To gain some perspective, she again took the Blind Spots Profile. While the Optimistic Image-Oriented Producer was still a strong influence, the Energetic New-Direction Risk Taker was becoming stronger.

Taylor now craved the excitement of new ideas and adventure. She preferred the excitement of considering many ideas over the results orientation of completed projects. The responsibility for two children also made her feel tied down, as much as she loved them. After some planning, Taylor decided to leave her corporate job and open a party-planning service, creating fun-filled occasions for children and adults. It was an entrepreneurial venture that was sourced by her new risk-taking self and the last bonus from her marketing job. She could operate it from home. Creating interesting ways for people to have fun made her feel excited.

What Influenced the Changes?

Did the changing situation bring out the Energetic New-Direction Risk Taker in Taylor, or did the emergence of a new part of her self drive her to change her life? Probably it was a bit of both. There's a chicken and egg relationships between how blind spots hiding emerging parts of ourselves interact with changes in our environment. The strange sensation Taylor felt signaled these new possibilities. If she had ignored them, she most likely would have experienced increasing stress and problems in her life—the way our blind spots get attention.

Taylor very much enjoyed her new life. She built upon the strengths of her previous work, using her results-oriented skills to provide the implementation energy for her business, which did very well. Within a few years, she had several employees to help. By year 10, Taylor's business was thriving.

As her children grew up, the party business started feeling routine. A new blind spot was beginning to emerge. Her inner voice was expressing new possibilities for Taylor's life that she wasn't quite ready to see. She experienced the shift as she became resistant to the constant details of executing events and felt less attracted to the constant interaction with people. Her enthusiasm was waning. She felt drawn to more introspective activities—yoga, meditation, time walking in the woods. Perhaps turning fifty was leading her to think more about herself.

Taylor began to clear the blind spot and recognize an emerging new voice. The Sensitive Perceptive Creator voice was becoming stronger. This voice is driven to find unique, creative ways of expressing the emotional needs of people. It spoke to Taylor through feelings, physical body sensations, and emotional memories. She tried for awhile to ignore it. The more she ignored it, the more she became tired, irritable, and exhausted. Finally, she decided to explore where it was leading. She observed which activities tired her out and which activities gave her a new sense of vitality.

Taylor recognized now that this voice had been there in her teens but she had chosen to ignore it, given the pressure for social achievement. Now she had time for exploration and took an art class. She began painting in her spare time. Her children had both left home and her husband was supportive. In fact he had found her difficult to live with as she struggled with feelings of disconnection from her party business. He encouraged her to go back to school for a degree in fine arts.

Taylor was able to sell her business for a good price, which more than funded her schooling. She developed her skills as a watercolor painter and became comfortable with a whole new set of goals for success.

While Taylor was coming to a new understanding of her self, she looked back at the changes in her life and observed the continuous threads that linked her choices: She had an inner passion for creating joy for herself and others. This she realized was the purpose of her life.

Directions from Your Self

Taylor's story reveals how life evolves through the discovery and clearing of blind spots. It is a process of continually removing the blinders that prevent us from seeing new possibilities for ourselves. We think we know who we are and what we want. Then we start to see blind spots that hide parts of ourselves that want to emerge. If we don't allow ourselves to see the possibilities these blind spots obscure, they *will* get our attention. We become irritable and out of sync. We meet obstacles. Our business collapses. Our marriages have problems. Our children become difficult to live with. Of course, blind spots are not the only cause of these difficulties. However, I very often see these signs in the lives of people who fail to clear a blind spot that screams of life potential.

The Inner Conflict

Another way of seeing our blind spots is the conflict that occurs between the social self and the essential self, which Martha Beck, author of *Finding Your Own North Star*, distinguishes. The essential self is the personality we are born with. The social self is the part of us that is developed in response to the people around us. Shaped by cultural norms and expectations, the social self moves us to strive, meets goals, sustains relationships, and seeks input from other people. These two selves continually negotiate with each other as we navigate daily life choices. To my way of thinking, a successful life is one where we are able to realize the potential of our essential self in ways the social self can build upon for broader purposes. This is what I refer to as *your highest and best purpose*.

So which self do you listen to? Listen to both but with attention to figuring out what the essential self is really saying. Since the essential self communicates via the emotional information pathways of physical feelings, you'll need to take the time to listen. If you don't relax and let that information come to you, you'll find the social self tries to takes over and a battle is waged. You will find that you have missed important meetings, forgotten significant deadlines, and feel heated emotions that have been stuck inside. This inner part of yourself will take its turn influencing your life, whether you choose to see it clearly or not!

As you manage these changes and recognize new challenges, you can step back and see the common threads that weave your life together. Your sense of purpose might be hiding behind the blind spots of confusion, conflict, and transitions. However, as you see new possibilities for yourself, your purpose will also emerge.

Emerging to Second Adult Life

One life transition that is gaining much attention these days is the shift to what I call *Second Adult Life*, a new life phase made possible by the longevity of today's baby-boomer population. While *First Adult Life* focused on responsibility for career, financial accumulation, family, and the needs of others, *Second Adult Life* redirects attention to new life possibilities that maximize personal satisfaction. Yet understanding what personal satisfaction means and channeling it into day-to-day plans requires time and a very new way of thinking and acting.

In designing coaching programs for those in the 55-year-old age group who are deciding whether to retire from their jobs, I learned that a common desire is *freedom* to emerge into a new way of living. Yet freedom has a wide range of meanings, some of which are very much related to personal blind spots. I counseled a man named Roger, who would find that freedom meant having the time to explore those areas of his life that had been hidden by the blind spots in his First Adult Life.

Roger, age 55 and CEO of a major financial institution, decided it was time to retire. When asked what he planned to do after work, he surprisingly said, "I have learned everything I want to know and don't want to learn another thing." For an active and enterprising man like Roger, this seemed a surprising response. Yet as I thought it through further and observed Roger, it made total sense. For his entire life, Roger had followed social expectations urging his achievement and responsibility. Finally he was creating the space to listen to a different voice.

Roger further explained his feelings: "People think because you are CEO that you run things the way you want to, that you always feel in control. But that's not the way power and leadership works. It's all about responsibility and concern over the demands and needs of board members, employees, shareholders, and customers. There isn't a moment in my day that I have been able to think about my needs in years. In fact, I'm not sure I would even know how to think about what I want. But I'm going to figure it out."

Part of what Roger was feeling was related to the wear and tear of his work. However, when he referred to not wanting to learn another thing, he was expressing a desire to leave intellectual pursuits behind for awhile. He wanted to fill his emotional needs, to rest and feel the freedom of no responsibilities.

Roger's Blind Spots Profile was the Reserved Analytical Strategist. In his work life he had been constantly using his mental gut strength. His blind spots showed when he distanced himself from others, which happened a great deal as his stress increased. Interestingly, when Roger did leave his job, he spent his unplanned days engaged in whatever activities his wife chose to do. He just wanted to be with her and share their time together without plans and responsibilities. He was putting his attention on his relationship with her.

In Second Adult Life, Roger was taking the time to discover a new side of himself. The topic of purpose added too much intellectualizing for his needs at this time. He was going to let his emotions lead the way. They were telling him in their own way how to find new purpose.

Toward Self-Actualization

In addition to developing a part of himself that had been hidden by a blind spot, Roger was going through the process of what psychologist Abraham Maslow described as hierarchy of needs. Maslow believed we must satisfy certain common inner-psychic human needs in the quest toward self-actualization. The first level requires that our physical needs for air, food, and shelter be met. The second level involves feeling safe and secure. The third level suggests companionship and affection—knowing that someone cares about us.

Self-actualization comes only when we find the role that we are suited to do, which brings us a sense of peace. For example, a painter must have creative expression. Roger needed to feel connected to *both* his intellect and emotions. The highest level of Maslow's model is when we operate with a sense of purpose and are growing, stretching, and using our highest gifts and talents.

Implicit in this notion of self-actualization is an understanding of life mission or purpose. Some people are fortunate to find their purpose in First Adult Life. Many others will make this a focus of Second Adult Life. As we see a Bill Gates leaving Microsoft and moving full-time into serving his foundation to erase global diseases, we see Second Adult Life purpose at work.

Find Your Purpose

Your life purpose may not as yet have unfolded for you. Early in your life, your purpose will be focused on learning about yourself and developing skills. As you acquire life experience and self-knowledge, you can see patterns in the types of challenges that engage you hinting at purpose. For example, aspects of your work may provide a way to use your strengths for impact beyond yourself. One thing is certain. Purpose is in action whether we recognize it or not. When we see behind the blind spots, we allow ourselves to accept life's changes and challenges with less turmoil and resistance. Life acts through us.

My life purpose is to help myself and others realize the potential of our innate personal talents and how to use them in our current settings. I've learned this as I see how I use my strengths most effectively in contributing to the lives of other people. What I do also brings me joy and a sense of personal satisfaction in my life.

What do you see as the purpose of your life today? Write a Statement of Purpose for your self to make it clear.

Your Statement of Purpose will be the last piece of information you supply to build your Personal Self-Portrait, which you been asked to add information to in each chapter. If you have answered these questions, you have gathered all the necessary material that will help you uncover blind spots and find your truest and most purposeful self. You are ready to build clear sight toward whatever goals you select to define your success. If you haven't answered these questions, you may want to wander back and answer them now.

In the final chapter, I want to help you take what you have learned and pass on the possibilities to others important to your life.

Pass the Possibilities

As we've read throughout this book, the sooner we open up the blind spots that cloud our view of our potential, the faster we can act upon opportunities that will energize and inspire us. When people see their blind spots and get clear sight, they often get excited about creating *pass-along* possibilities: They want to help every person who affects their work and life to develop clear sight, for example:

- Everyone wants to learn the blind spots of spouses and children to improve relationships at home.
- Bosses want everyone who reports to them to identify their blind spots to reduce the stress of the work group.
- Peers want to get their colleagues into blind spot identification so the team can be more collaborative and more enjoyable to work with.
- Top executives want whole work groups to learn about their blind spots to help the culture become less stressful and more productive.

When all of these people drop the defensiveness that holds their blind spots in place and get balanced feedback from those around them, all kinds of fresh possibilities emerge for working together constructively.

The curiosity and interest people have in this work were made obvious when I was getting a make-up consultation for a video. Six women sat on high chairs on either side of me as I conversed with the cosmetologist about blind spots. Slowly other conversations stopped as attention focused on the subject of my video. Finally the women on the end of the row said loudly, "Could you speak up, we're having trouble hearing down here!"

I laughed to myself as the group of us talked about blind spots of husbands, children, best friends, and relatives that create frictions in relationships. These women wanted to influence *everyone else's* blind spots. That's a very common response. It's always easier to see other people's blind spots than our own.

I remember one business client named Mia who was considering a first marriage at the age of 45. She was wrestling with the pros and cons of the relationship and decided she couldn't move forward until I had done a blind spots analysis of her future potential husband. Mia wanted to know in advance what the potential frictions would be in this relationship. I explained that this would be a conflict of interest for me, and an intrusion into his personal affairs—thinking that would put the matter to rest.

Shortly Mia came back and told me that her potential husband, Steve, wanted to meet with me. He, too, was concerned about the potential marital problems. I set ground rules in advance: I would speak to him on a confidential basis. Nothing that occurred in that discussion would be communicated back to Mia by me. Any further discussion would take place between Mia and Steve.

I met with Steve who was interested in learning about his blind spots, especially about how they related to his work as an undercover detective. We also talked about the kind of blind spots that might show up in a personal relationship. However, I wouldn't discuss a word about Mia. That was for him and Mia to do together. I can, however, report that Mia and Steve have been happily married for several years!

Talking with Others About Blind Spots

Talking about blind spots with important people in your life and work can open doors to understanding. However, like the situation with

Mia and Steve, clear boundaries need to be respected and the right climate set in advance if the conversation is to be constructive. Here's some advice.

Talk About Blind Spots First in a Work Context

Discussion of blind spots may be sensitive for people. However, when a blind spot is an obstacle to someone's promotion or raise, the individual may be more motivated to face it. For example, a spouse may express concern about interpersonal roadblocks in a marriage with his or her mate for years without action. Yet when these same blind spots stand in the way of a significant promotion, the mate may leap to solve them.

During the American Revolutionary War, the Marquis de Lafayette observed the competition and goal orientation of this culture: He noted that if there were a line to the guillotine, Americans would all be fighting to be first, so driven were they to succeed. Competition and striving to be number one at work lead Americans to do many things, even consider their blind spots.

I remember one man whose wife and staff had been telling him for years to relax because his stress was driving them crazy. When his boss pointed out the stressful behavior as a block to a senior vice president title, the man enthusiastically sprang into action. He was paradoxically *driven to relax*, doing everything possible to change his behavior. He took walks, practiced new ways of talking with his staff, changed the way he answered the phone, and was disciplined to change a whole range of habits. After three months, he appeared like a new person talking and acting totally at ease. He got the promotion, and as a by-product changed his relationship with every member of his family for the better!

However, take caution: While the desire for achievement at work can drive people to consider their blind spots, the competition and judgment involved in standard setting often influence people to retreat from blind spots discussion. This goes to the heart of the principles of clear sight, which are very helpful to keep in mind in discussing someone else's blind spots. Let's review them.

Shift to Neutral

When we feel judged or critiqued, we retreat to the comfortable behaviors that hold our blind spots in place. Remember Stephen in Chapter 6, who went from bottom to top of the group in his scores on a company 360° feedback report. When I asked him what had made the difference in the work we had done together, he answered, "I know exactly what it was. You allowed me to see myself without judgment, and with that I was able to make conscious choices."

That is the meaning of the first principle of clear sight: Shift to Neutral. To consider your own blind spots, you need to be able to do this. To talk with someone else about their blind spots, you must help both of you shift to neutral. Otherwise, they may shut down and turn away.

If you've ever had the opportunity to work with adolescents, you can see this phenomenon clearly. Adolescents are so sensitive to judgment that they recognize your nonverbal cues before you open your mouth. If your posture communicates judgment, they will close the discussion before it begins. I've seen them withdraw from discussion in the middle of a sentence.

No doubt about it. You have to approach a discussion of someone else's blind spots from a neutral perspective with *joint* goals in mind.

Imagine Positive Possibilities

In talking with someone about their blind spots, it also helps to focus on the positive possibilities. Let's be honest. If you initiate a conversation with someone else about their blind spots because you want to change something they do that bothers you, the discussion is really about you. That works totally against the goal of helping the individual to feel safe enough to discuss their own blind spots.

Start a talk about blind spots with a discussion about what a person's strengths bring to your relationship. That shifts the conversation to neutral and imagining positive possibilities. We can reach mutual agreement far faster when we recognize one another's strengths than when we start pointing out weaknesses.

If you want to discuss someone else's blind spots, start by talking about your own and identify some positive possibilities for mutual benefit. For example, "I want to talk about the positive things our relationships does for my sense of well-being. I think the way I express stress may be working against that lately and I want you to help me see how I might change that."

In this way, I am recognizing strengths and putting my own blind spots out for discussion first. It's natural for the other person to follow suit if they are comfortable with the approach. You are also in a positive position to open discussion of whether they would want to discuss a blind spot that you see.

Simply Focus on Success

Always think about blind spots in relation to a shared goal. It may be that someone's old habit of monopolizing conversations, for example, upsets every aspect of your relationship. That's too big a hurdle to overcome initially for success. Instead, focus on a joint project you are doing like giving a party. Then address the strengths and potential blind spots each member of the group brings to that task.

For example, in giving a party your strengths come out in decorating the table and setting up. Your blind spots show up in timing the cooking and trying to entertain guests at the same time. Fortunately your party-planning partner has a strength in overseeing cooking and a blind spot in having to converse with the crowd. You break down tasks in ways that complement each other.

You will have better chances for success when you take small steps that build possibilities for future work.

Stretch Your Strengths

You use your own strengths to build up areas that blind spots obscure. Help someone else to follow this approach. If someone whose gut strengths are in the mental arena doesn't recognize your feelings sufficiently, help them to learn the right questions to ask you to get feeling information from you. If someone whose gut strength in the feeling arena is smothering you in a discussion of feelings, help the individual to get a conceptual framework for looking at the mental and instinctive side of things.

Keep your expectations modest. Don't expect someone else to change. Help them to use what they already do well to build strength in an area obscured by blind spots.

Choose with Confidence

When we turn our blind spots into strengths, we feel and act more confidently. We bring the assessment of our capabilities for doing something into balance with the feelings we have about those capabilities. The thinking side and feeling side of our brain are coordinated to work together.

In approaching others about their blind spots, start from a place of confidence within yourself. Wayne Dyer says quite profoundly in his Introduction to the book *Ask and It Is Given*, "When you change the way you look at things, the things you look at change." When you bring your confidence to people who are uneasy about discussing their blind spots, they sense your confidence and you may begin to feel more confidence resonating from them. They may begin to integrate information from both sides of their brain in engaging you.

You must reach out with confidence to help someone else feel confident.

Sharing Perspective on Blind Spots

When you talk with someone else about the mutual blind spots that can affect your relationship, you both need objective information to share. I've presented you with several models you can use for this purpose: the Blind Spots Profile and Blind Spots 360, the Five Most Common Blind Spots Framework, and the Old Habits Blind Spots grid. They can help you to focus your discussion.

Informal discussion of blind spots among a small group of people can be helpful. Discussion of blind spots among members of a working team is often very useful. A good starting point is to identify a shared team goal. Have group members complete the Blind Spots Profile and Blind Spots 360, drawing information from other members of the team. In the shared discussion, each team member can be asked to identify the strengths and blind spots they want to work on in pursuing the shared team goal. This builds realistic expectations for team member contributions and can identify any group blind spots at work.

However, groups that include competitors or people in authority relationships with one another may require some special help. These dynamics may interfere with a shift to neutral perspective. It's probably best to use a facilitator to help structure these conversations.

This facilitator could be a human resource specialist, coach, or consultant who can bring a neutral perspective and make sure to keep the discussion within safe boundaries. You may also want to utilize such an individual for assistance with particularly difficult blind spot related issues.

How can you choose a professional that is right for you and your situation?

Criteria for Selecting Professional Support

You'll want to carefully consider the credentials and experience of professionals you choose to work with you on your blind spots. Here are four key areas to explore:

1. *Demonstrated Experience*
   Does this person have demonstrated experience working with blind spots in environments similar to yours? What are their results in helping people like you to recognize blind spots and turn them into strengths? Can they give you references?
2. *Nonjudgment*
   Does this person make you feel valued and not judged? Do you feel you can talk with this person without their telling you what to do? Are you comfortable that this person can give you balanced feedback

in a way that you can be open to receiving it? Is the person supportive but tough enough to stand up to you when you don't agree with
what they are saying?

3. *Confidentiality*

What assurances do you have that your discussions will be confidential? Does the individual work for any individuals that could be a
conflict of interest for you? What does the individual do with any
data or assessment instruments gathered on your behalf?

4. *Education and Certification*

What is the person's training? Have they completed certifying programs or certificates? Are they licensed to do their work? Do they
have an advanced degree in counseling, psychology, or a related field?
What supervision did they receive before going into practice on
their own?

For example, coaches often receive training from the Coaches
Training Institute (CTI) or the International Coaching Federation
(ICF), which offers several levels of certification. Career counselors
and psychologists are often licensed by their state and certified by
their professional organization. Each professional specialty has certain philosophies and orientations that may be important for you to
consider. Ask about them.

Imagine a World with Clear Sight

What possibilities do I see when I work with individuals, groups, and organizations who take the work of building clear sight seriously?

It is a world of confident, productive people who achieve goals and
results without feeling the stress and wear and tear of those who remain
blind-sighted. They know their strengths and continually open any blind
spots. They regularly update their plans for clear sight.

This group of people sees endless possibilities for success and joy in
their work and personal lives. They recognize a sense of purposefulness
in what they do and achieve the career aspirations they set out for
themselves. These people use their analytical and emotional brains to
reach a balanced perspective on their actions and plans and are not

afraid to reconsider their decisions when their feelings suggest a change in course.

Moreover, they take risks and admit mistakes, always reaching out to get a balanced perspective on their strengths as well as the opportunities to improve what they do. They know how to give balanced feedback to others.

These people know how to connect with one another and create a positive resonance to support their work. They also respect each other and acknowledge differences. They establish constructive boundaries for their discussions and are not afraid to raise issues and concerns that will make relationships more productive and satisfying.

They work hard but know how to create a sense of balance in their work and personal lives. Without that balance they realize how stress and lack of energy can slow down their effectiveness. They also build circles of family and friends that share their sense of purposefulness and resilience.

These are the people we call *successful* in the twenty-first century.

Appendix

Descriptions of All Tools

Tools	*Where Found*
(in order of their introduction in the book)	
Five Most Common Blind Spots Framework	Sample Framework on page 10. A tool for self-identification of blind spots introduced in Chapters 1 and 2.
Clear Sight Plan	A statement of two or three steps that keeps you aware of what you need to do to turn your blind spots into strengths; introduced in Chapters 1 and 2. Included as part of cases throughout the book.
Personal Self-Portrait	Information useful to identifying blind spots, which you are asked to gather about yourself by answering a question at the end of each chapter. The Personal Self-Portrait is introduced in Chapter 1 and explained in more detail in Chapter 3.

Priority for Handling Blind Spots Grid	Sample Grid on page 32. Introduced in Chapter 3, this tool helps you identify which blind spots merit attention and which require more fact-finding.
Blind Spots Profile	Blind Spots Profile Matrix on page 44. Descriptions of the Nine Models pages 45–47. A tool for self-identification of blind spots, which is introduced in Chapter 4.
Blind Spots Profile Online	Description on page 57. Same tool introduced in Chapter 4 available through an online questionnaire at www.whatsmyblindspot.com.
Blind Spots 360	Description on pages 56–57. A tool for finding out how other people see your blind spots, which is introduced in Chapter 5 and available for group use. See www.whatsmyblindspot.com for more information.
Discussion Format: How Do You See My Strengths and Blind Spots?	Format on page 60. Discussion guide introduced in Chapter 5 for use in one-on-one discussions to get someone else's view on your strengths and blind spots.
The Confidence Triangle	Triangle on page 106. Tool presented in Chapter 10 to help you identify the source of personal blindspots. Used in a number of the clear sight strategy stories.
Statement of Strengths	Introduced in Chapter 11. A tool for self-identifying one's core strengths including gut strengths that provide confidence at work.

Old Habits Blind Spots Grid	Sample Grid on page 132. A tool introduced in Chapter 12 for self-identifying blind spots that you have held for a long time.
Characteristics of Disconnection	List on page 168. Tool used in Chapter 15 to identify behaviors that interfere with connection and communication with others.
Group Blind Spots Finder	Finder on page 188. Tool introduced in Chapter 17 to identify the blind spots of a group including issues of culture, thinking style, gender, race, religion, disability, ethnicity, age, economic status, or sexual orientation.
Statement of Purpose	Tool introduced in Chapter 18 to identify the central focus of your life, which may not become clear until you have sufficient life experience to observe the continuity and commitment to what you do.

The Five Most Common Blind Spots Framework

One way of analyzing your blind spots is to think through how each of these five most common blind spots may show up in your work.

Misused Strengths	A strength you use too little or too much. Example: too much entertaining or performing and not enough disciplined communicating.
Old Habits	Relying on old behaviors that made you successful in the past, which no longer are effective.

Stress Expressed	How your behavior affects others when you are under stress. Example: distracted behavior or late assignments cause others frustration.
Untuned Radar	Ignoring nonverbal cues you give and receive. Example: an angry posture; not recognizing the cues and resonance others feel from your presence.
Disconnect	Ignoring factors important to communication. Example: not listening or engaging others.

	I See It	I Don't See It
Others See It	Box 1: Ready to Attack	Box 2: Need Other's Input
Others Don't See It	Box 3: Update Your Personal Self-Portrait	Box 4: Explore Discomfort

Priority for Handling Blind Spots Grid:
Who Sees My Blind Spots?

Quick Thinking Style

	Read Feelings First	Read Ideas First	Read Instincts First
Extroverted	Optimistic Image-Oriented Producers (Page 224)	Energetic New-Direction Risk Takers (Page 225)	Assertive Get-It-Doners (Page 226)
Interpersonal	Warm Relationship Builders (Page 226)	Practical Questioning Loyalty Builders (Page 227)	Responsible High-Standards Builders (Page 228)
Introspective	Sensitive Perceptive Creators (Page 229)	Reserved Analytical Strategists (Page 230)	Empathic Conflict-Avoiding Diplomats (Page 231)

Quick Feeling Style

Blind Spots Profile Matrix

Blind Spots Profile

Descriptions of the Nine Models

Optimistic Image-Oriented Producers

Quick Thinking Style: read feelings first.

Quick Feeling Style: extroverted.

Greatest Personal Strength: High-energy multitasker, produces many projects valued by others.

Potential Blind Spot: Constant multitasking can lead to disorganization and indecision. When pressured can become distant and alienate others.

The Optimistic Image-Oriented Producer gets things done and involves people in his plans by constantly telling others about what he is doing. In school we saw these people as head of the class, teams, and activities. The more they accomplish, the more they feel highly regarded. Their Quick Thinking Style tunes them into how what they are doing affects the feelings of other people. For this reason we often see them in marketing, communication, or image producing roles. Their Quick Feeling Style supports their giving directions to others in ways that carry their image of what needs to be done into action. They are also tuned into the feelings of what motivates others to act.

When people who identify with this model operate with blind spots, they will start so many projects that they get disorganized, overwhelmed, and indecisive. While normally confident, optimistic, and motivating to others, these blinded individuals can become distant and alienate others. If this happens over the long haul, they will lose confidence, get tuned to their negative feelings, and become self-defeated. By slowing down, setting priorities and thus gaining clear sight, they regain perspective to effectively accomplish what they want to do.

Energetic New-Direction Risk Taker

Quick Thinking Style: read ideas first.

Quick Feeling Style: extroverted.

Greatest Personal Strength: Constantly initiating new ideas. Enthusiasm creates energy and excitement.

Potential Blind Spot: Lack of self-disciplined follow-through on ideas can lead to failure. When feeling boxed in by structure, can become irritable, blaming, and lose memory for recent events and decisions.

The Energetic New-Direction Risk Taker is exciting to be around and responds with enthusiasm to any new idea presented. In school, we often saw these people caught up in the energy of outside school adventures and activities, as they found the routine of schoolwork to be boring and mundane. Their Quick Thinking Style tunes them into how what they are thinking can be communicated to other people around them. Since they are usually extroverted in feeling style, they will tell everyone in sight about a new idea that captures their attention. Then another new idea comes along and they forget that the previous idea ever existed. The practice of living in the moment comes naturally to these individuals.

They can make great entrepreneurs as they generate energy about new ideas, and they feel very comfortable operating without a game plan. To be successful they need to have people or an organization behind them that can structure, pin down, and implement their ideas.

When operating with blind spots, they get so caught up in new idea generation that they ignore the structure and discipline needed to implement their ideas. This can lead to blame and criticism of others, when the source of the problem may lie in their own lack of structure and disciplined focus on implementation. When they gain clear sight, they slow down, get organized, set priorities, and focus on getting things done.

Assertive Get-It-Doner

Quick Thinking Style: think instincts first.

Quick Feeling Style: extroverted.

Greatest Personal Strength: Knows how to get things done.

Potential Blind Spot: Can become too confrontational or bossy. When unappreciated can become suspicious and mistrustful.

Put an Assertive Get-It-Doner in the middle of a chaotic group of people who don't know how to get organized and in just a few minutes the chaos will begin to clear. This individual uses Think Instincts First perception to understand the capabilities and operational nature of people, and with this sensory input knows just how to make people and organizations work to get something done. With an Extroverted Quick Feeling style, he or she is able to communicate an easy game plan and get others going. Often having a strong physical presence, these people seem to know the most efficient way to meet their goals.

They are interested in power and control, which they usually seem to have a good instinctive sense to manage. When they operate with blind spots, they can become so assertive that they can alienate others. When others push back hard in response to their assertiveness, they can become suspicious and feel unappreciated. By expressing a softer, less controlling side they are able to gain clear sight and reconnect with others.

Warm Relationship Builder

Quick Thinking Style: read feelings first.

Quick Feeling Style: interpersonal.

Greatest Personal Strength: Innate understanding of the feelings and needs of others.

Potential Blind Spot: When feelings not reciprocated appropriately, they can withdraw and focus on their personal shortcomings. Can try to avoid negative feelings by becoming manipulative to get the appreciation they desire.

When you meet a Warm Relationship Builder, you feel their interest and focus on being with you. They have a gift for connecting with others, and use that gift to build businesses and causes that are responsive to people. Their Quick Thinking Style of Read Feelings First orients them to other people's personal needs and feelings, and uses this knowledge to understand others. Their Quick Feeling Style of interaction reinforces this engagement. In fact, if you watch the Relationship Builder interacting, you will often see him unconsciously taking on the body positions of the person he is talking with, a natural way of expressing empathy. These people can effectively network and build relationships that make things happen.

When Warm Relationship Builders are not appreciated by others over the long term, their blind spots can show. They withdraw and feel less confident. They may also unconsciously try to manipulate others to express appreciation for them, for example, doing some act to get attention. By articulating their needs and concerns more directly to others, they gain the clear sight to use their interpersonal skills effectively.

Practical Questioning Loyalty Builder

Quick Thinking Style: read ideas first.

Quick Feeling Style: interpersonal.

Greatest Personal Strength: Uses intellect to test the dependability and trustworthiness of organizations and people they work with.

Potential Blind Spot: Can work so hard to test the trustworthiness of a person or organization that they lose confidence and put off decisions.

The Practical Questioning Loyalty Builder uses a Quick Thinking Style of Read Ideas First and an Interpersonal Quick Feeling Style. This means a focus on constant testing and debate of their ideas about the people, organization, and causes they commit to serving. Doubtful of the reliability of managers or leaders until they have a chance to test their ability, these individuals will constantly evaluate the merits of any program, project, or person with which they are involved. They want to test others before committing to them. Once they feel an individual is reliable, they will persevere and sacrifice. They are practical, responsible, and can make effective managers and leaders.

When their blind spots show, these people can get overly caught up in questioning and debate. Unable to trust people or an organization, they procrastinate on decisions. To gain clear sight, they need to bring their keen intellect and scrutinizing questions into focus, trust themselves, and make clear choices. Their balanced leadership and commitment to goals leads to effective action.

Responsible High-Standards Builder

Quick Thinking Style: read instincts first.

Quick Feeling Style: interpersonal.

Greatest Personal Strength: Innate self-discipline and standards for doing the right thing for the organization.

Potential Blind Spot: In pursuit of goals can become too serious and overly responsible. Can become distant, angry, aloof, and inflexible when too focused.

The Responsible High-Standards Builder has a strong inner sense of how to do things the right way. Whether it is building a marketing plan, a financial statement, a new organization, or any other product or process, this individual will seek high standards and goals for doing it right. Their style of Think Instincts First tunes them into understanding the capabilities and operational nature of people, and with this sensory input they know just how to lay out a plan to get things done well. Their Interpersonal Quick Feeling Style drives them to express their understanding in interaction with others. Thus, they both naturally understand and can explore ways with others on how to set standards that will help to achieve demanding goals. Attaining their goals in a way close to their standards gives them a sense of well-being.

Responsible High-Standards Builders are often solid leaders of established organizations or groups, where their attention to standards reinforces a strong operation. They have to be careful, however, that their blind spot of focusing too much on their standards and thus decreasing flexibility doesn't demotivate others and lead to micromanaging. They also need to keep their anger in check when others disregard their efforts toward perfection. With clear sight these people have the flexibility, energy, and commitment to goals that create high standards that can adapt to changing conditions.

Sensitive Perceptive Creator

Quick Thinking Style: read feelings first.

Quick Feeling Style: introspective.

Greatest Personal Strength: Uses perception to find unique, creative ways of contributing to others and understanding the emotional needs and state of people and organizations.

Potential Blind Spot: Can become too emotionally focused and ignore social expectations. Can overwork and become ill.

The Sensitive Perceptive Creator understands the deep meaning of events, people, or situations. They are often found in communication, writing, or artistic expression, or in psychology, counseling, or cultural studies. Their Read Feelings First Thinking Style and Introspective Quick Feeling Style lead these people to process the feelings of day-to-day interactions through deep introspection and put forth an understanding of human events that is often not readily available to other individuals. The intensity of this process can lead this individual to a sense of isolation and emotionality. However, since their feeling process is so introspective, others may have no knowledge that the Sensitive Perceptive Creator is experiencing such intensity when others view outside demeanor.

Sensitive Perceptive Creators can bring a unique perspective to organizations, particularly in areas such as marketing, communications, and management development. They themselves need to be particularly aware of their potential blind spots of too much inward emotional focus, which can lead to isolation or burnout. Taking time out to balance their intense natural emotional process is important for clear sight.

Reserved Analytical Strategist

Quick Thinking Style: read ideas first.

Quick Feeling Style: introspective.

Greatest Personal Strength: Insightful methodical ability to see both forest and trees.

Potential Blind Spot: Can move too much into the head and become distant and aloof. When pressed can become distracted and dictatorial.

The Reserved Analytical Strategist has a unique ability to step outside a problem or system and methodically review both the strategy and details of the entire situation, and present an insightful perspective. He uses his Ideas First Quick Thinking Style and Introspective Quick Feeling Style to absorb and articulate solutions that are usually unique and have been thought through with greater depth than most people would naturally provide. These individuals prefer to remain emotionally reserved as this gives them the neutral perspective they need to support their in-depth mental process.

When people who identify with this model operate from blind spots, they can become distant and aloof and ignore other's needs for more personal discussion and connection. They can also become so caught up in their ideas that they can sometimes talk for long periods about something when others would be happy with a short answer. The good thing is that the Reserved Analytical Strategists are usually responsive to feedback when they allow the time for it. For clear sight, they can recognize these blind spots and be sure to develop the social interaction and empathy needed to be effective in relationships.

Empathic Conflict-Avoiding Diplomat

Quick Thinking Style: read instincts first.

Quick Feeling Style: introspective.

Greatest Personal Strength: Uses perception to "walk in the shoes" of others and understand their needs. Make excellent facilitators to bring a group together.

Potential Blind Spot: Can become lost in other people's needs and ignore their own. Avoid negative feedback.

The Empathic Conflict-Avoiding Diplomat can be a valued member of any work team when he uses his innate ability to walk in the shoes of others to initiate ways that resolve conflicts, problems, and turmoil. Using his Read Instincts First Thinking Style, this individual has an inner sense of the capacity and nature of people. Combined with a Feeling Style of Introspection, this individual will have probed the essence of how people can operate together in the most harmonious way possible. Desiring a peaceful environment in which to work for himself, he is troubled by confrontation, conflict, criticism, or demands that upset his natural pace and approach to doing things.

The introspective world of an Empathic Conflict-Avoiding Diplomat may be hard for others to comprehend. Like other Introspectives, this individual does a lot of his processing within himself so others are only aware of a small part of his daily thinking. Blind spots occur when these people are overpressured or stressed, and they lose track of their connection to themselves. In this state they can become overly sensitive to criticism and can lose the discipline that keeps their lives in order. Clear sight brings the structure and support that help these people make a major difference in the functioning of any organization or team, simply by the gestures they make from understanding those around them so well.

Blind Spots Finder Tools Online

The Blind Spots Profile and the Blind Spots 360 are online tools that provides a starting point for discussions about your blind spots. To access these tools go to www.whatsmyblindspots.com. Throughout the book, the results of these two tools are discussed as part of stories about individuals who gain clear sight.

Blind Spots Profile Online

The Profile Online includes 110 questions and takes 15 to 20 minutes to take. It will help you get a picture of your gut strengths and related blind spots following the same nine Blind Spots Profile models presented in Chapter 4. You will receive an online printout of how strongly your responses suggest you identify with each of the nine models described on pages 224–231. Your results give you a starting point for discussion of your strengths and blind spots.

Blind Spots 360

The 360 provides an online tool for groups to use to gather feedback about yourself from between 3 and 15 people, including yourself. You will receive a printout report, which you can compare and contrast to the Blind Spots Profile results. The Blind Spots 360 is organized around the Five Most Common Blind Spots Framework found on page 10.

Discussion Format: How Do You See My Strengths and Blind Spots?

1. What do you see as my greatest personal strength?
2. What do you see as my greatest personal strength in relationships?
3. In terms of how I handle stress, is there anything I do that creates more stress for others?
4. If we met for the first time, what impression would you have of me before I had said a word?

5. Some people read information very quickly. Have you noticed how I grasp information (e.g., gut reactions, intuitive feel, getting a quick overview)? Have you noticed any ways that I miss nonverbal information?
6. In terms of my communication with other people:
   - Am I approachable?
   - How do I engage others?
   - How do I manage differences of opinion?
   - Do I recognize contributions of others sufficiently?
   - Am I socially and politically aware?
7. Are there any blind spots you think I may not see about myself that affect my relationships with other people?

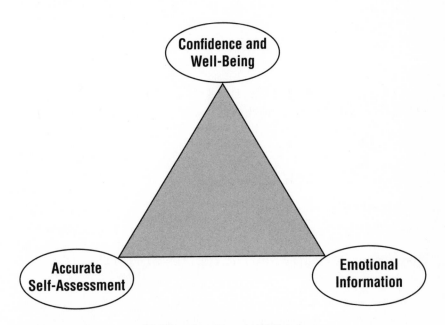

Accurate self-assessment of skills and
abilities combined with positive emotional
information about those capabilities increases
confidence and well-being.

The Confidence Triangle

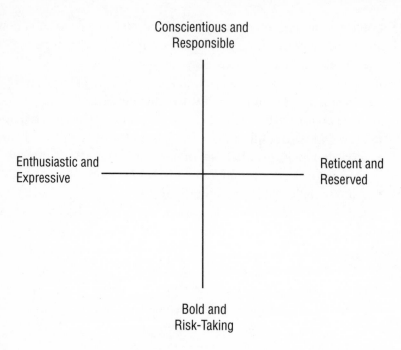

Conscientious and
Responsible

Enthusiastic and
Expressive

Reticent and
Reserved

Bold and
Risk-Taking

Old Habits Blind Spots Grid:
Do You Overdo Your Strengths in Any of the Four Grid Directions?

Characteristics of Disconnection

When we develop blind spots, we lose sight not only of our words and their impact on others, but of the overall nature of our relationships. With diminished connection to one another, we all lose out in the process. This disconnection results when we:

- *Appear unapproachable*. Seeming unapproachable, untrustworthy, or uncomfortable with other people, we make others feel we aren't interested in what they have to say.
- *Disengage*. Not speaking clearly, not listening to what others have to say, not providing useful feedback, we may not present our ideas convincingly.

- *Ignore the contributions of others.* Taking credit for what others do, we don't communicate how we value what they do and get lost in our own agendas.
- *Act judgmentally or create conflict.* Judging other people or igniting issues that create ill will lead to conflict and disconnection.
- *Lack social skills.* Not reaching out to people because they are junior to us, or not taking the time to understand others, shifting blame: These behaviors destroy relationships.

Group Blind Spots Finder

1. In which of the following areas, if any, do you feel the group may have beliefs or blind spots that could affect you in reaching your goals with this group? Check the appropriate boxes.

    _____ culture   _____ style of thinking or learning
    _____ gender   _____ race
    _____ religion   _____ ethnicity
    _____ disability   _____ age
    _____ economic status   _____ sexual orientation

2. What belief(s) do you feel the majority of the group members hold that could influence your effectiveness in reaching your goal?

3. How would this belief specifically influence or limit your effectiveness?

4. What specific steps can you take to increase your possibilities for success?

Notes

Chapter 1   *See Blind Spots*

Dennis W. Bakke, *Joy at Work* (Seattle, WA: PVG, 2005).

Malcolm Gladwell, *Blink: The Power of Thinking Without Thinking* (New York: Little, Brown and Company, 2005).

Paul D. Tieger and Barbara Barron-Tieger, *Do What You Are* (Boston: Little, Brown and Company, 1995).

Chapter 2   *Develop Clear Sight*

Arthur L. Williams, "Believe It's Possible," in Jack Canfield, *The Success Principles: How to Get from Where You Are to Where You Want to Be* (New York: HarperCollins Publishers, 2005).

Chapter 3   *Can You See What They See?*

Stephen Covey, *The Seven Habits of Highly Effective People* (New York: Fireside, 1990). Part 1 provides an interesting chapter on personal paradigm.

Trevor Gandy, cited in "Invisible Resume Has Real Value," *Hartford Courant* (January 23, 2006).

Daniel Goleman, *Working with Emotional Intelligence* (New York: Bantam Books, 1998).

Chapter 4   *Model Yourself*

Isabel Briggs Myers and Peter Myers, *Gifts Differing* (Palo Alto, CA: Consulting Psychologist Press, 1980).

Helen Palmer. *The Enneagram* (San Francisco: HarperSanFrancisco, 1991).

Janet Levine, *The Enneagram Intelligences* (Westport, CT: Bergin & Garvey Paperback, 1999).

Chapter 6   *Shift to Neutral*

J. Paul Getty, quoted in Jack Canfield, Mark Victor Hansen, and Les Hewitt, *The Power of Focus* (Deerfield Beach, FL: Health Communications, Inc., 2000).

Daniel Goleman, *Working with Emotional Intelligence* (New York: Bantam Books, 1998), Chapter 4, "The Inner Rudder."

Manager self-assessment: Richard Boyatsis, *The Competent Manager: A Model for Effective Performance* (New York: John Wiley & Sons, 1982).

Antonio Damasio, *The Feeling of What Happens* (New York: Harcourt Brace, 1999).

Study of high performers: Diane Nilsen and David Campbell, "Self-Observer Rating Discrepancies: Once an Overrater, Always an Overrater?," *Human Resource Manager* (Summer/Fall 1993).

Chapter 7   *Imagine Positive Possibilities*

Daniel Gilbert, *Stumbling on Happiness* (New York: Alfred A. Knopf, 2006).

Robert Allen, "Release the Brakes" in Jack Canfield, *The Success Principles* (New York: HarperCollins, 2005).

Jim Collins, *Good to Great* (New York: HarperCollins, 2001).

Martin Seligman, *Learned Optimism: How to Change Your Mind and Your Life* (New York: Alfred A. Knopf, 1991).

The reference to Richard Davidson's research is from Daniel Goleman, *Working with Emotional Intelligence* (New York: Bantam Books, 1998), Chapter 5.

Chapter 8 *Simply Focus on Success*

Napoleon Hill, *Think and Grow Rich* (New York: Random House, 1960).

Facts on importance of financial goals and reference to work of Dr. Amy Wrzesniewski, His Holiness the Dalai Lama and Howard C. Culter, M.D., *The Art of Happiness at Work* (New York: Riverhead Books, 2003).

Why people work statistics: 2006 MetLife Employee Benefits Trend Study, *Executive Insider* (March 13, 2006).

Department of Labor statistics: Tom Rath and Donald O.Clifton, *How Full Is Your Bucket?* (New York: Gallup Press, 2004).

Abby Ellin, "Was Earning That Harvard M.B.A. Worth It?" *New York Times* (June 11, 2006).

"I Have One Life and It Must Come Together," *Inc.* magazine (October 2003), 60.

Malcolm Gladwell, *Blink* (New York: Little, Brown and Company, 2005).

Chapter 9 *Stretch Your Strengths*

Entrepreneurs: Ann Graham Ehringer, *Make Up Your Mind* (Los Angeles: Merritt Publishing, 1995).

Brain functioning: "The Sources of Gut Feelings" in Daniel Goleman, *Working with Emotional Intelligence* (New York: Bantam Books, 1998).

Emotional brain: Albert Mehrabian study in Robert K. Cooper and Ayman Sawaf, *Executive EQ: Emotional Intelligence in Leadership and Organizations* (New York: Perigree Books, 1998).

Henry Reed and Brenda English, *The Intuitive Heart* (Virginia Beach, VA: A.R.E. Press, 2000).

Shafica Karagulla, *Breakthrough to Creativity* (Marina del Ray, CA: De-Vorss and Company, 1967).

Elaine N. Aron, *The Highly Sensitive Person* (New York: Broadway Books, 1997).

Jack Canfield, Mark Victor Hansen, and Les Hewitt, *The Power of Focus* (Deerfield Beach, FL: Health Communications Inc., 2000).

Chapter 10   *Choose with Confidence*

On confidence: Mike Krzyzewski, *Leading with the Heart* (New York: Warner Business Books, 2000).

Chapter 11   *Identify Strengths*

Marcus Buckingham and Donald O. Clifton, *Now, Discover Your Strengths* (New York: Free Press, 2001).

Stephen Covey, *The Eighth Habit* (New York: Free Press, 2004).

Antonio Damasio, *The Feeling of What Happens* (New York: Harcourt Brace, 1999).

Belle Linda Halpern and Kathy Lubar, *Leadership Presence* (New York: Gotham Books, 2004).

Student strengths: Claudia Marshall Shelton and Robin Stern, Ph.D., *Understanding Emotions in the Classroom* (Port Chester, NY: National Professional Resources, 2004).

Chapter 12   *Check Old Habits*

Tom Markert, *You Can't Win a Fight with Your Boss* (New York: Harper-Collins Publishers, 2005).

Marie G. McIntyre, *Secrets to Winning at Office Politics* (New York: St. Martin's Griffin, 2005).

Chapter 13   Address Stress

Paul Connelly, Human Resource Measurement, www.PerformancePrograms
.com web site, March 12, 2006.

Monica's stress patterns: a useful instrument to identify underlying blind
spot related stress patterns is the Hogan Development Survey. See
www.PerformancePrograms.com for more information.

David Allen, Getting Things Done: The Art of Stress-Free Productivity
(New York: Penguin Books, 2003).

Jim Loehr and Tony Schwartz, The Power of Full Engagement (New York:
Simon & Schuster, 2003).

Research studies: Mishlove, J., "Intuition: The 'X' factor in Business,"
Journal of Creativity, 1995, and F. Marton, P.J. Fensham, and S.D.
Chaiklin, "A Nobel's Eye View of Scientific Intuition: Discussions
with the Nobel Prize Winners in Physics, Chemistry, and Medicine,
1970–1986," International Journal of Science Education 16 (February
1996): 65. Found in Robert K. Cooper and Ayman Sawaf, Executive
EQ (New York: Perigree Trade Paperback, April 1998).

Chapter 14   Tune Radar

Dale Carnegie, How to Win Friends and Influence People (New York:
Pocket Books, 1982).

Robert K. Cooper and Ayman Sawaf, Executive EQ (New York: Perigree
Trade Paperback, April 1998).

Chain damping: A. Mcgee-Cooper, You Don't Have to Come Home from
Work Exhausted (New York: Bantam, 1992), pages 245–262 found in
Robert K. Cooper and Ayman Sawaf, Executive EQ (New York: Peri-
gree Trade Paperback, April 1998).

Dan Goleman, Annie McKee, and Richard Boyatisis, Primal Leadership
(Boston: Harvard Business School Press, 2002).

Richard Boyatis and Annie McKee, Resonant Leadership: Renewing Yourself and Connecting with Others Through Mindfulness, Hope and Com-
passion (Boston: Harvard Business School Press, 2005).

Chapter 15   *Connect*

Rosamund Stone Zander and Benjamin Zander, *The Art of Possibility* (New York: Penguin Books, 2002).

Don Miquel Ruiz, "Speak with Impeccability," in Jack Canfield, *The Success Principles* (New York: HarperCollins, 2005).

Keith Ferrazzi, *Never Eat Alone* (New York: Currency Doubleday, 2005).

Debra Fine, *The Fine Art of Small Talk* (New York: Hyperion, 2005).

Tim Sanders, *The Likeability Factor* (New York: Crown Publishers, 2005).

Chapter 16   *See* Their *Way*

Peter Senge, *The Fifth Discipline Field Book: Strategies and Tools for Building a Learning Organization* (New York: Doubleday, 1994).

Case history of Continental: Daniel Goleman, *Working with Emotional Intelligence* (New York: Bantam Books, 1998), Chapter 12, "Taking the Organizational Pulse."

Chapter 18   *Find Purpose Over Time*

Richard L. Leider, *The Power of Purpose* (San Francisco: Berrett-Koehler Publishers, 1997).

Viktor E. Frankl, *Man's Search for Meaning* (New York: Washington Square Press, a division of Simon & Schuster, 1984).

Martha Beck, *Finding Your Own North Star* (New York: Three Rivers Press, 2001).

Abraham Maslow, *Motivation and Personality*, 3rd ed. (New York: Addison-Wesley, 1987).

Chapter 19   *Pass the Possibilities*

Esther and Jerry Hicks, *Ask and It Is Given: Learning to Manifest Your Desires* (Carlsbad, CA: Hay House, Inc., 2004).

Additional Resources

WE ARE CONSTANTLY providing new information about seeing blind spots and finding clear sight.

Please check out our web site at www.whatsmyblindspot.com for information about training programs, speeches, and other tools that can help you work and live blind spot free!

The Blind Spots School	A one-day program followed by a period of one-on-one coaching by phone to identify your blind spots and put a Clear Sight Plan into action that will help you to reach your goals.
Workshops	Group workshops are available for organizations or working teams to identify individual and group blind spots that can be affecting your goals and to develop Clear Sight Plans.

Speeches

Claudia Shelton presents both fun and insightful customized keynote speeches on a range of topics related to Blind Spots and Clear Sight including:

- Leadership.
- Change Management.
- Career and Professional Development.
- Motivation and High Performance.

Index